NATIONAL DEFENSE RESEARCH INSTITUTE

T0210380

THE RAND SECURITY COOPERATION PRIORITIZATION AND PROPENSITY MATCHING TOOL

Christopher Paul | Michael Nixon | Heather Peterson | Beth Grill | Jessica Yeats

Prepared for the Office of the Secretary of Defense

The research described in this report was prepared for the Office of the Secretary of Defense (OSD). The research was conducted within the RAND National Defense Research Institute, a federally funded research and development center sponsored by OSD, the Joint Staff, the Unified Combatant Commands, the Navy, the Marine Corps, the defense agencies, and the defense Intelligence Community under Contract W91WAW-12-C-0030.

Library of Congress Cataloging-in-Publication Data is available for this publication.

ISBN: 978-0-8330-8098-1

The RAND Corporation is a nonprofit institution that helps improve policy and decisionmaking through research and analysis. RAND's publications do not necessarily reflect the opinions of its research clients and sponsors.

Support RAND—make a tax-deductible charitable contribution at www.rand.org/giving/contribute.html

RAND® is a registered trademark.

Cover design by Pete Soriano

RAND OFFICES
SANTA MONICA, CA • WASHINGTON, DC
PITTSBURGH, PA • NEW ORLEANS, LA • JACKSON, MS • BOSTON, MA
DOHA, QA • CAMBRIDGE, UK • BRUSSELS, BE
www.rand.org

Preface

Security cooperation remains a key line of effort for the U.S. Department of Defense. Traditionally, security cooperation has been an area in which predicting success is difficult, but increasing fiscal constraints have amplified pressure for greater efficiency. Recent research has made progress in identifying conditions and approaches most likely to lead to security cooperation success. This research effort developed a diagnostic tool that enables a preliminary assessment of the match between a partner's (or a potential partner's) propensity for security cooperation success and current (or planned) investment in—or priority for—that partner, with the goal of identifying possible mismatches for further scrutiny and policy analysis. The tool is available online at http://www.rand.org/pubs/tools/TL112.html. The audience for this report is likely limited to those who plan, prioritize, or allocate resources for U.S. security cooperation efforts or those who are interested in such efforts.

This research was sponsored by the Office of Cost Assessment and Program Evaluation in the Office of the Secretary of Defense (OSD[CAPE]) and conducted within the International Security and Defense Policy Center of the RAND National Defense Research Institute, a federally funded research and development center sponsored by the Office of the Secretary of Defense, the Joint Staff, the Unified Combatant Commands, the Navy, the Marine Corps, the defense agencies, and the defense Intelligence Community.

For more information on the International Security and Defense Policy Center, see http://www.rand.org/nsrd/ndri/centers/isdp.html or contact the director (contact information is provided on the web page).

Contents

Figures and Tables

Figures

Tables

Summary

Security cooperation is the umbrella term used to describe a wide range of programs and activities "conducted with allies and friendly nations to build relationships that promote specified U.S. interests, build allied and friendly nation capabilities for self-defense and coalition operations, [and] provide U.S. forces with peacetime and contingency access."[1] These activities remain an important line of effort for the U.S. Department of Defense (DoD), but increasing pressure on defense spending provides a new imperative to get the most possible benefit out of security cooperation efforts whose overall scope and budget are likely to decrease. Thus, it will be important for DoD to scrutinize and perhaps reevaluate existing and proposed security cooperation efforts with partner nations (PNs) to ensure that the expected benefits align with cost and corresponding policy prioritization.

Recent RAND research identified practices and contextual factors associated with greater or lesser degrees of success in security cooperation. That assessment was based on systematic analyses of 29 historical case studies of U.S. efforts to build partner capacity since the end of the Cold War.[2] Building partner capacity (BPC) is a complicated endeavor that takes place in complex and nuanced environments, but the study found that there are some clear best approaches to BPC, clear best traits for desirable partners, and clear best practices for recipient partners. The results demonstrate that when an effort is consistently funded and delivered, supported and sustained, well matched to partner capabilities and interests, and shared with a partner that supports it and is healthy economically and in terms of governance, prospects for effectiveness are very good. The results also suggest that BPC can still be effective when only some practices are followed or when only some conditions are met. BPC done well, done consistently, and matched to partner absorptive capacity and interests can be effective even when the partner is not particularly robust in any dimension at the outset.

The findings, presented in the RAND report *What Works Best When Building Partnership Capacity and Under What Circumstances?* (MG-1253/1-OSD), serve as a base of evidence to inform policy discussions and investment decisions. Not surprisingly, the strongest and most consistent correlations found were for factors related to the alignment of interests and the matching of capacity-building activities to partner objectives and to the ability of the PN to absorb and retain the materiel and training provided. The criticality of these seam, or match-

---

[1] See Defense Security Cooperation Agency, "Frequently Asked Questions (FAQs)," web page, last updated August 15, 2012.

[2] Christopher Paul, Colin P. Clarke, Beth Grill, Stephanie Young, Jennifer D. P. Moroney, Joe Hogler, and Christine Leah, *What Works Best When Building Partnership Capacity and Under What Circumstances?* Santa Monica, Calif.: RAND Corporation, MG-1253/1-OSD, 2013.

ing, factors inspired the overriding metaphor and single summary recommendation from the earlier RAND study: "Find the right ladder, find the right rung."

The study identified the following nine specific and measurable factors with strong correlations with BPC effectiveness in the 29 cases, four of which are under U.S. control:

1. spending more money on BPC or undertaking more BPC initiatives
2. ensuring consistency in both the funding and implementation of these initiatives
3. matching BPC efforts with PN objectives and absorptive capacity
4. including a sustainment component in the initiatives.

Four factors are characteristics of the partner or are under PN control:

5. PN invests its own funds
6. PN has sufficient absorptive capacity
7. PN has high governance indicators
8. PN has a strong economy.

One factor is shared between the United States and the PN:

9. PN shares broad security interests with the United States.

The correlation observed between these nine factors and BPC success, as well as the pattern of factors present and absent in the 29 case studies, provided both the inspiration and the empirical foundation for the current effort. This research extends beyond the earlier study in both depth and breadth by asking the following questions:

- Which of the rest of the countries in the world have patterns of factors that correspond with success in historical cases?
- Which other factors can be identified in the literature that might contribute to propensity for success in this area?

We used MG-1253/1-OSD and other existing research to provide a firm foundation of received wisdom, permitting a more systematic and global decision-support process for security cooperation prioritization and resource allocation than has previously been available.

The RAND Security Cooperation Prioritization and Propensity Matching Tool

Building on these prior research efforts, this report describes a preliminary diagnostic tool developed from global public-use data sets to systematically assess the propensity for successful U.S. security cooperation in any country in comparison with current (or planned) security cooperation funding levels and priorities. The RAND Security Cooperation Prioritization and Propensity Matching Tool is a diagnostic tool built in Microsoft Excel® that will help DoD decisionmakers preliminarily identify mismatches between the importance of a country to U.S. interests, U.S. security cooperation funding to that country, and the propensity for successful U.S. security cooperation with that country. For each of the world's 195 countries, the tool produces an overall security cooperation propensity score. These scores can then be compared with U.S. security cooperation funding levels and country prioritization.

The tool includes 27 constructs drawn from hypotheses and evidence about factors that might increase or decrease the effectiveness of security cooperation, according to the existing literature; this is the analytic core of the tool. Each construct has an associated weight representing strength in terms of propensity for effective security cooperation and the strength of the research contributing to that construct. We then grouped the 27 constructs into ten categories to present the information in a more succinct way.

Each of the 27 constructs is represented by one or more measures or proxies. There are 66 measures in total (presented in Appendix A of this report), derived from publicly accessible databases with global or nearly global coverage. All data sources are included in the list at the end of this report and in the relevant tabs of the tool spreadsheets themselves.

So, for each of the 195 countries, the tool provides an overall security cooperation propensity score, which aggregates the propensity scores for ten categories. These categories summarize results for 27 constructs, which synthesize one or more of a total of 66 measures. Figure S.1 portrays this relationship visually.

The tool is designed to be reusable and updated by a generalist user (i.e., someone who is familiar with basic Excel). To this end, the team sought data sources for the measures that are publicly available and would be updated regularly. The tool was populated with the most current publicly accessible data in 2012, and it includes instructions for users to update the

Figure S.1
Relationships Between the Layers of the Tool

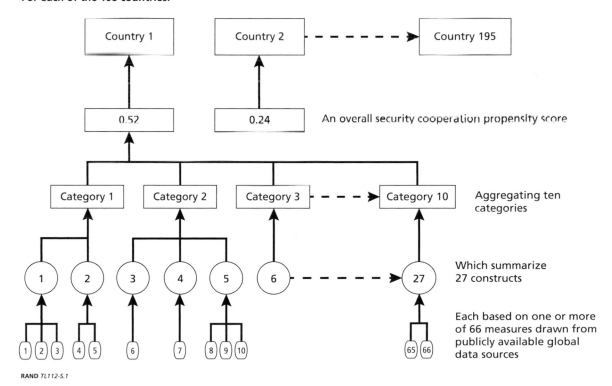

currency of the source data as needed; additional instructions are provided in Appendix D of this report.

The RAND Security Cooperation Prioritization and Propensity Matching Tool is a preliminary diagnostic device that has the virtues of being systematic, being based on global data, and not relying on subjective assessments. It provides a starting point for asking sometimes-hard questions about the relationship between U.S. security cooperation funding, U.S. priorities, and the likelihood of success in specific countries. It is not a substitute for strategic thought, however. There is no one-size-fits-all, automated approach to choosing one set of countries that should get funding and another set that should not. The purpose of the tool is to highlight potential mismatches for further study and, perhaps, to identify areas of concern to be addressed as part of that inquiry.

Acknowledgments

The authors are grateful for the support and help of many individuals. In particular, we would like to thank our principal sponsor point of contact, Tom Johnson in OSD(CAPE), for his insight and guidance. We also wish to thank the following government officials who supported this project and the earlier research that it builds upon: Matthew Schaffer, David Lowe, Timothy Bright, and Melissa Kirkner in OSD(CAPE); Maureen Bannon and Aaron Jay in the Office of the Under Secretary of Defense for Policy; James Miner at the Defense Security Cooperation Agency; and CAPT Connie Frizzell, CAPT John Sniegowski, and CDR John Mann of the Joint Staff (J5).

We are also grateful for the assistance provided by our RAND colleagues. Terrence Kelly offered initial guidance and help with project formulation. Angela O'Mahony made herself available for multiple consultations over the course of the project. Finally, Colin P. Clarke, Stephanie Young, Jennifer D. P. Moroney, and Joe Hogler provided advice based on their participation in earlier research and help with the comparative case studies. Quality assurance reviewers John Peters and Bradley Wilson provided valuable feedback that helped us improve the report. Lauren Skrabala drafted the summary and edited the final document.

Abbreviations

BPC	building partner capacity
COCOM	combatant command
DoD	U.S. Department of Defense
FIPS	Federal Information Processing Standard
FY	fiscal year
GDP	gross domestic product
ISO	International Organization for Standardization
OSD(CAPE)	Office of Cost Assessment and Program Evaluation, Office of the Secretary of Defense
PN	partner nation
SFA	security force assistance
SIPRI	Stockholm International Peace Research Institute
SME	subject-matter expert
USAID	U.S. Agency for International Development

CHAPTER ONE

Introduction: Prioritizing Security Cooperation

Background

Security cooperation is the umbrella term used to describe a wide range of programs and activities "conducted with allies and friendly nations to build relationships that promote specified U.S. interests, build allied and friendly nation capabilities for self-defense and coalition operations, [and] provide U.S. forces with peacetime and contingency access."[1] Security cooperation activities remain an important line of effort for the U.S. Department of Defense (DoD):

> Since the United States assumed the role of a leading security provider after the end of World War II, DoD has worked actively to build the defense capacity of allied and partner states . . . . These efforts further the U.S. objective of securing a peaceful and cooperative international order. . . . In today's complex and interdependent security environment, these dimensions of the U.S. defense strategy have never been more important. U.S. forces, therefore, will continue to treat the building of partners' security capacity as an increasingly important mission.[2]

However, increasing pressure on defense spending after more than a decade of war provides a new imperative to get the most possible benefit out of security cooperation efforts. This fiscal pressure, coupled with DoD's efforts to "rebalance toward the Asia-Pacific region,"[3] provides an opportunity to scrutinize and perhaps reevaluate existing and proposed security cooperation efforts with individual partner nations worldwide to ensure that the expected benefits of these efforts align with the cost required to realize those benefits and their corresponding policy prioritization.

Traditionally, efforts to evaluate likely benefits relative to priorities for security cooperation have taken place at the country level and have depended almost entirely on individual country subject-matter experts (SMEs). Unfortunately, these SME assessments have often suffered from one or more of the following shortcomings:

- *Lack of comparability across countries.* Each country has a different SME or set of SMEs, and they use context-specific (or just different) standards.

---

[1] See Defense Security Cooperation Agency, "Frequently Asked Questions (FAQs)," web page, last updated August 15, 2012.

[2] U.S. Department of Defense, *Quadrennial Defense Review Report*, Washington, D.C., February 2010.

[3] U.S. Department of Defense, *Sustaining U.S. Global Leadership: Priorities for 21st Century Defense*, Washington, D.C., January 2012a, p. 2.

- *Lack of impartiality.* SMEs often have an interest or stake in the country on which they focus and thus end up advocating for security cooperation and other resources rather than acting as impartial assessors.
- *Variation in quality of expertise and extent and quality of advocacy.* Reasons include the level of experience, level of knowledge, and the personalities of different SMEs.

Thus, efforts to take a portfolio view of the balance and priorities for security cooperation often stumble, with the individual country SME-based process aggregating awkwardly or decisions being based on strength of expertise or strength of advocacy rather than effective comparative analysis.

Recent RAND research, presented in the report *What Works Best When Building Partner Capacity and Under What Circumstances?* (MG-1253/1-OSD), identified both practices and contextual factors associated with greater or lesser degrees of success in security cooperation. That assessment was based on systematic analyses of 29 comparable cases (see Chapter Two).[4] Coupled with other research in this area (see the discussion in Chapter Three), there is a firm foundation of received wisdom regarding effectiveness in security cooperation that can inform a more systematic and global decision-support process for security cooperation prioritization and resource allocation than has previously been available.

Purpose of This Project

This research sought to create a tool that applies the received wisdom on security cooperation to data from global public-use data sets to systematically make diagnostic assessments of the propensity for successful U.S. security cooperation in every country in the world in comparison with current (or planned) security cooperation funding levels and priorities. While the results are intended to serve as preliminary diagnostic assessments and admittedly lack country-level nuance, the tool described here does avoid the three challenges associated with SME-based individual assessments: lack of comparability, lack of impartiality, and variation in quality and advocacy.

Preview of Results

The RAND Security Cooperation Prioritization and Propensity Matching Tool is a diagnostic tool built in Microsoft Excel® that will help DoD decisionmakers preliminarily identify mismatches between the importance of a country to U.S. interests, U.S. security cooperation funding to that country, and the likelihood that the United States will be successful in achieving its objectives vis-à-vis that country. The tool contains data for the world's 195 countries on 66 measures that inform 27 constructs in ten categories and produce an overall security cooperation propensity score for each country. These scores can be compared with U.S. security

---

[4]   Christopher Paul, Colin P. Clarke, Beth Grill, Stephanie Young, Jennifer D. P. Moroney, Joe Hogler, and Christine Leah, *What Works Best When Building Partnership Capacity and Under What Circumstances?* Santa Monica, Calif.: RAND Corporation, MG-1253/1-OSD, 2013.

cooperation funding levels and country prioritization.[5] The main contribution of the tool is that it estimates the likelihood that security cooperation will be effective with a given country for every country in the world.[6] In addition, it gives users the ability to easily compare countries on a range of factors and measures related to security cooperation. Data sources in the baseline tool are current through 2012. The tool includes instructions for users to update the currency of the source data as needed.

Organization of This Report

This report describes how the tool was developed and provides an overview of the tool itself, as well as suggestions and cautions for its use. The theoretical foundation for the tool comes largely from earlier RAND research presented in the 2013 report *What Works Best When Building Partner Capacity and Under What Circumstances?*[7] Chapter Two provides a brief summary of the results of that research.

Chapter Three describes the development of the tool, beginning with the process the study team used to identify existing hypotheses regarding security cooperation effectiveness, distill those hypotheses to a series of constructs, group those constructs into ten categories, assign measures to each of the constructs, and weight the constructs based on the quality of evidence supporting the hypotheses they represent and the quality of data available to represent them. Further, it provides a brief overview of the mathematical modeling used to operationalize the tool and the case studies used to validate the tool, which are described in more detail in Appendixes B and C.

Chapter Four offers a detailed description of the tool, which is available as a downloadable Excel file at http://www.rand.org/pubs/tools/TL112.html. It provides an overview of the spreadsheets in the tool and instructions for adjusting the weights of the constructs for different applications or for sensitivity analysis. Additional detail on how to update the spreadsheet is included in Appendix D. Chapter Five concludes the report by offering some recommendations for the use of the tool, some cautions about possible misuses of the tool, and suggestions for further research.

---

[5] A country's level of importance or priority is determined by U.S. policymakers and derived from strategic guidance. Country prioritization is based on classified guidance and is not included in the unclassified tool but can be added (and updated) by the user.

[6] It is important to note that the accuracy of the estimate is limited by the quality of available research and global quantitative measures, and current estimates are largely devoid of country-specific nuance. Still, as a preliminary security cooperation portfolio diagnostic assessment mechanism, the tool has the virtues of being systematic, comprehensive, and independent of input from individual country-level analysts.

[7] Paul et al., 2013.

CHAPTER TWO

Foundational RAND Research: What Works Best When Building Partner Capacity and Under What Circumstances?

The core of the theoretical foundation for this effort and the RAND Security Cooperation Prioritization and Propensity Matching Tool comes from the 2013 RAND report *What Works Best When Building Partner Capacity and Under What Circumstances?* (MG-1253/1-OSD). That report includes detailed individual and comparative analyses of U.S. efforts to build partner capacity in 29 countries since the end of the Cold War. This chapter provides a summary of methods and findings from that research. We combined these findings with results from a broader range of security cooperation–related research to build the model that underlies the tool (as described in Chapter Three).

A Note on Terminology

Security cooperation is the umbrella term used to describe a wide range of programs and activities "conducted with allies and friendly nations to build relationships that promote specified U.S. interests, build allied and friendly nation capabilities for self-defense and coalition operations, [and] provide U.S. forces with peacetime and contingency access."[1] Related to, and clearly within the realm of security cooperation, are several related terms of art, all falling under the broader tent: security assistance, building partner capacity, and security force assistance.

- *Security assistance* consists of "a group of programs, authorized by law that allows the transfer of military articles and services to friendly foreign governments."[2] The U.S. strategy for security assistance is set forth as a multi-year plan developed by the U.S. Department of State and coordinated with key elements of DoD.
- *Building partner capacity* (BPC) is a generic term used to describe efforts to build the security and defense capabilities of partner countries, which will enable them to make valuable contributions to coalition operations and subsequently improve their own capabilities.[3]

---

[1] See Defense Security Cooperation Agency, 2012.

[2] U.S. Department of Defense, *Security Assistance Management Manual (SAMM)*, Washington, D.C., DoD 5105.38-M., April 30, 2012. A full list of security assistance programs can be found on p. 33 of the manual.

[3] U.S. Department of Defense, 2010; U.S. Department of Defense, *Building Partnership Capacity: QDR Execution Roadmap*, Washington, D.C., May 22, 2006.

- *Security force assistance* (SFA) is defined as "DoD activities that contribute to unified action by the [U.S. government] to support the development of the capacity and capability of foreign security forces and their supporting institutions."[4]

The earlier RAND report used the term *building partner capacity*, while this report uses the term *security cooperation*. We recognize security cooperation as the broader, parent term but do not mean to make any significant mention of the residual part of security cooperation that is not part of BPC, nor do we wish to attempt to specify it. While acknowledging that the various terms in this area denote slightly different (if predominantly overlapping) sets of activities or areas of emphasis, we leave the lexical hair-splitting to others and use *security cooperation* and *building partner capacity* interchangeably in this chapter and the next.

Data and Evidence Used in the Prior Research

The earlier RAND report also considered and compared historical case studies of U.S. efforts to build partner capacity in order to generate a base of evidence to inform policy discussions and investment decisions, comparing the results of U.S. BPC efforts since the end of the Cold War for 29 selected partner nations (PNs). By examining 20 years of data on 29 systematically selected countries, the RAND team was able to build a solid foundation of evidence on the effectiveness of different features of capacity-building efforts under different conditions and in different contexts.

Because the United States provided some kind of security cooperation funding for BPC activities in 184 countries between 1990 and 2010, the RAND team could not conduct case studies for every instance of BPC support during that span. Cases were selected based on three criteria: First, we identified for exclusion all "high-end" partners; second, we identified priority partners (based on target spending thresholds); finally, we identified countries that had conducted at least two external deployments of at least company strength between 1990 and 2010 (and, thus, may have plausibly and observably demonstrated capacity built). After excluding high-end partners, the RAND team added all countries that were identified as very-high-priority countries based on historical funding levels, followed by high-priority countries that deployed externally at least twice. This produced the list of the 29 countries studied. Further details of case selection can be found in MG-1253/1-OSD.[5] Each country case was divided into between two and four chronological phases. These phases served as the unit of analysis for the study. The average length of a phase was eight years, though some were much shorter or longer. Phase changes were not intended to reflect small-scale changes or changes on a single factor; rather, they indicate significant shifts and events affecting many factors (or perhaps a smaller number of particularly important factors) in the overall case. Each case also included a baseline phase from which to calculate changes.

For each phase, the RAND team identified a set of inputs within a certain context that produced certain outcomes. Patterns of these input, contextual, and outcome factors constituted evidence in the study. Each phase of each case included approximately 75 different input, contextual, or outcome factors, and each case included a detailed narrative. Together, these

---

[4] U.S. Department of Defense Instruction 5000.68, *Security Force Assistance (SFA)*, October 27, 2010, p. 18.

[5] See Paul et al., 2013.

data supported two types of analyses: (1) single-case lessons learned with discursive examples and (2) comparative or aggregate analysis across phases and cases. We used this evidence to test a series of literature-derived hypotheses and determined whether it supported or failed to support these hypotheses.

Summary of Findings from the Prior Research

BPC is a complicated endeavor that takes place in complex and nuanced environments, but the earlier RAND study found that there are some clear best approaches for those conducting BPC, clear best traits for desirable partners, and clear best practices for recipient partners. The study results demonstrate that when all three have been followed, effectiveness has ensued. That is, if BPC is consistently funded and delivered, supported and sustained, well matched to partner capabilities and interests, and shared with a partner that supports the effort and is healthy economically and in terms of governance, prospects for effective BPC are very good. The results also suggest that BPC can still be effective when only some practices are followed or when only some conditions are met. BPC done well, done consistently, and matched to partner absorptive capacities and interests can be effective even when the partner is not particularly robust in any dimension at the outset.

The strongest and most consistent correlations found in that, however, were for factors at the seam of U.S. and PN control—factors related to the alignment of interests and the matching of capacity-building activities to PN objectives and to the ability of the PN to absorb and retain the materiel and training provided. The criticality of these seam or matching factors inspired the study's overriding metaphor and single summary recommendation: "Find the right ladder, find the right rung."

Of greatest relevance to the current effort, MG-1253/1-OSD identified nine specific and measurable factors with strong correlations with BPC effectiveness in the 29 cases studied. Four of these factors are under U.S. control:

1. spending more money on BPC or undertaking more BPC initiatives
2. ensuring consistency in both the funding and implementation of these initiatives
3. matching BPC efforts with PN objectives and absorptive capacity
4. including a sustainment component in the initiatives.

Four factors are characteristics of the partner or are under PN control:

5. PN invests its own funds
6. PN has sufficient absorptive capacity
7. PN has high governance indicators
8. PN has a strong economy.

One factor is joint between the United States and the PN:

9. PN shares broad security interests with the United States.

The correlation observed between these nine factors and BPC success, as well as the pattern of factors present and absent in the 29 case studies, provided both the inspiration and the empirical foundation for the current effort.

Moving from Nine Key Findings to a Global Model

In briefing results of the earlier research to project sponsors, questions arose about the possibility of using the key findings—the nine factors correlated with positive BPC outcomes—as part of a prognostication tool with which to at least preliminarily assess prospects for success in current or future BPC efforts. As a way to demonstrate (and partially test the prospects for) such an application, the RAND team prepared a table showing the patterns of presence or absence of the nine factors for the most recent phase of each of the 29 cases studied, along with whether or not BPC in that phase had been effective. All factors (including effectiveness) were scored in a binary fashion: 0 = absent, 1 = present. This table is duplicated as Table 2.1. For visual discrimination, absent factors have been shaded in red and present factors shaded in green.

Table 2.1 shows that not only are these nine factors individually correlated with BPC success across all phases of the 29 cases, but their sum is a relatively strong predictor of BPC success in the latest phase of each case. In every case in which the sum of the nine positive factors was four or less (cases 25–29), BPC was assessed as less effective. Every case in which seven or more of the nine factors were present exhibited effective BPC. Most of the cases with either five or six of the nine factors (highlighted in yellow in the table) were successful, but one, in particular, was not. This suggests a turning point (i.e., some minimally sufficient number and strength of positive factors in place) and is, perhaps, an indication that additional factors might be important in predicting BPC effectiveness.

On the whole, however, Table 2.1 points to a promising implementation of that earlier research, and other research of its kind, by asking two questions:

- Which of the rest of the countries in the world have patterns of factors that correspond with success in historical cases?
- Which other factors can be identified in the literature that might contribute to propensity for success in this area?

These two questions motivated this research effort. The simplest possible implementation of the earlier findings to meet sponsor requirements would have been to somehow score the nine factors for every country in the world, making a simple binary prediction based on the presence or absence (or prospects for presence or absence) of the nine factors. Several things led us to a different (and more complicated) course. First, while the factor scores for the 29 case studies are binary, they were not derived using simple formulae incorporating quantitative data; rather, the scores were based on holistic interpretations of qualitative and quantitative data as part of a set of rich case narratives. Collecting these narratives for each country in the world would have both exceeded the resources available to the project and run afoul of the project mandate for a tool that did not rely on expert assessments. To include these factors, we needed to find proxy measures to represent them, which involved further methodological scrutiny. Second, while the report was pathbreaking in the depth and scope of its analyses, numerous other studies have contributed to the accumulated received wisdom on

Table 2.1
Summary of Case Studies, Factors, and BPC Effectiveness

Case	Spent/did more	Consistency in funding and providing BPC	BPC matched PN objectives and absorptive capacity	BPC included a sustainment component	PN invested its own funds	PN had sufficient absorptive capacity	PN had high governance indicators (WBGI in top two-thirds)	PN had strong economy (GDP top 50th percentile)	Shared PN and U.S. security interests	Sum of positive indications	BPC in last phase assessed as effective
1	1	1	1	1	1	1	1	1	1	9	1
2	1	1	1	1	1	1	1	1	1	9	1
3	1	1	1	1	1	1	1	1	1	9	1
4	1	1	1	1	1	1	1	1	1	9	1
5	1	1	1	1	1	1	1	1	1	9	1
6	1	1	1	1	1	1	0	1	1	8	1
7	1	1	1	1	1	1	1	0	1	8	1
8	1	0	1	1	1	1	1	1	1	8	1
9	1	0	1	1	1	1	1	1	1	8	1
10	1	1	0	1	1	1	1	1	1	8	1
11	1	0	1	1	1	1	1	1	1	8	1
12	1	1	1	0	1	1	1	1	1	8	1
13	0	1	1	1	1	1	1	1	1	8	1
14	1	1	0	1	1	1	1	1	1	8	1
15	1	0	1	1	1	1	1	1	1	8	1
16	1	0	1	1	1	1	0	1	1	7	1
17	1	0	1	1	1	1	0	1	1	7	1
18	1	0	1	0	1	1	1	1	1	7	1
19	1	1	1	0	0	1	1	1	1	7	1
20	1	0	1	0	1	1	1	1	0	6	1
21	1	1	1	0	1	0	1	0	1	6	1
22	1	0	0	1	1	1	0	1	1	6	1
23	0	0	1	1	1	1	1	0	1	6	0
24	1	1	1	0	0	0	0	1	1	5	1
25	1	0	0	0	0	1	1	1	0	4	0
26	1	0	0	0	0	1	0	1	0	3	0
27	1	0	0	0	0	0	0	1	0	2	0
28	0	0	1	0	0	0	0	0	1	2	0
29	1	0	0	0	0	0	0	0	0	1	0

NOTE: The table is sorted based on the descending sum of positive indicators. WBGI = World Bank Governance Indicator.

security cooperation, and we would be remiss if we failed to at least try to include insights from others in the tool. This led us to expand the aspirations of the project from a simple mechanical application of the original RAND study results into a broader undertaking, described in Chapter Three.

Research and Tool Development

The chapter describes the process through which we developed the RAND Security Cooperation Prioritization and Propensity Matching Tool. Again, the purpose of the tool is to help planners identify possible mismatches between the priority of or funds spent on security cooperation and the prospects that security cooperation will be effective. The tool's primary contribution is its utility as a model for the propensity for security cooperation to be effective in a given country, based on historical studies of security cooperation and the broader existing literature on security cooperation effectiveness.

Backward Modeling

The tool is essentially a quantitative model for predicting propensity for security cooperation in individual countries based on a host of input or contextual factors. Traditionally, researchers would build such models with large quantities of past data and then project or extrapolate the model onto new data, with attendant concerns about the generalizability of the model.[1] The process followed here is somewhat outside that traditional paradigm. Rather than building a model based on traditional statistical analyses of a robust historical data set, we built our model based on a single, smaller data set (that used in MG-1253/1-OSD) and a collection of findings from other research drawn from very small databases (often either single case studies or "small-n" comparative studies). *Then* we applied those findings to a robust global data set.

Because the robust quantitative data set does not enter the process until the very end, we have described the process in briefings as a sort of "backward" modeling, in which the theory, received wisdom, and assumptions come first and the data are subjected to them, rather than drawing received wisdom from a single large data set and projecting those results onto other data. In some sense, our process can be described as a kind of Bayesian modeling approach, with the model itself being entirely part of the assumptive prior distribution.[2] The remainder

---

[1] See one of the many discussions of such issues in William R. Shadish, "The Logic of Generalization: Five Principles Common to Experiments and Ethnographies," *American Journal of Community Psychology*, Vol. 23, No. 3, June 1995.

[2] Bayesian refers to the Reverend Thomas Bayes, who worked on early 18th-century problems in calculating odds when gambling and for what would now be called actuarial calculations for insurance. Bayesian analysis endeavors to estimate parameters of an underlying distribution based on the observed distribution, beginning first with a "prior distribution," which may be based on anything, and making cumulative calculations with actually observed data, resulting in a "posterior distribution." The results depend on both the observed data and the assumed distribution of the prior distribution and the strength with which the assumption is held (the weight it is given). Bayesian analysis is somewhat controversial because the validity of the result depends on how valid the prior distribution is, and this cannot be assessed statistically. For a more

of this chapter describes that modeling processes, detailing how we identified the elements and strength of our prior beliefs and ordered them into the model for the tool.

Foundation in the Literature

To distill the received wisdom on security cooperation and populate our Bayesian prior distribution, we sought strong results in the existing research. Unfortunately, very few studies have systematically assessed the historical effectiveness of security cooperation across multiple countries. Rather than rely exclusively on a small number of quantitative studies, the RAND team conducted a wide-ranging literature review and catalogued hypotheses related to security cooperation effectiveness.

The team began by sorting through the vast literature on security cooperation to identify studies and documents that specifically addressed security cooperation effectiveness. Sources included RAND, the Congressional Research Service, the Institute for Defense Analyses, *Foreign Affairs*, and the *Defense Institute of Security Assistance Management Journal*, as well as government documents, such as Army Field Manual 3-07, *Stability Operations*, and the Joint Center for International Security Force Assistance *Commander's Handbook for Security Force Assistance*. The full list of more than two dozen studies can be found in the bibliography.

The team reviewed the studies to identify hypotheses related to security cooperation effectiveness. A hypothesis was anything that a study suggested might either increase or decrease the effectiveness of security cooperation. For example, having low institutional capacity might make it harder for a country to absorb security cooperation support and, as a result, make security cooperation with that country less likely to be successful. The team identified more than 100 separate hypotheses related to the effectiveness of security cooperation.

Some studies had only a few hypotheses, while others had more than a dozen; most fell somewhere in the middle. There were several hypotheses that showed up in multiple studies in slightly different forms. For example, many studies suggested that security cooperation would be more effective with PNs that have good governments and/or shared interests with the United States. Other hypotheses showed up just a few times. For example, only one study suggested that a PN that had successfully implemented U.S. security cooperation efforts in the past was likely to do so in the future, though that hypothesis makes a lot of intuitive sense.

For each contributing study, we collected and compiled the tested hypotheses or assertions. Further, with a Bayesian modeling process in mind, we also collected information on the proposed strength of the relationship or correlation, and we made a holistic assessment of the quality or strength of the research and empirical foundation for those results, used later in the process to determine weights (as described later in this chapter). Table 3.1 provides a notional example of what our preliminary literature review produced, listing the source study, the thesis or hypothesis, the strength of the relationship claimed (either a specific correlation or regression coefficient, or general language about strength of relationship), and our assessment of the study, including both a letter grade and a brief description of the empirical foundation.

---

detailed discussion, see Andrew Gelman, John B. Carlin, Hal S. Stern, and Donald B. Rubin, *Bayesian Data Analysis*, Boca Raton, Fla.: Chapman and Hall, 1995.

Table 3.1
Notional Example of Literature Review Hypothesis Collection and Evaluation Process Results

Study	Hypothesis	Strength of Correlation	Quality of Research
Study 1	Hypothesis 1	Statistically significant (+0.5)	A: empirical, 29 case studies, 20 years
Study 1	Hypothesis 2	Statistically significant (−0.25)	A: empirical, 29 case studies, 20 years
Study 1	Hypothesis 3	Statistically significant (+0.3)	A: empirical, 29 case studies, 20 years
Study 2	Hypothesis 1	"Important"	C: lessons learned, 3 cases studies
Study 2	Hypothesis 2	"Important"	C: lessons learned, 3 cases studies
Study 3	Hypothesis 1	None stated	C: synthesis of SME advice
Study 3	Hypothesis 2	None stated	C: synthesis of SME advice
Study 3	Hypothesis 3	None stated	C: synthesis of SME advice

Sifting the Hypotheses

Not all hypotheses on security cooperation effectiveness that the team collected were useful for the tool. After gathering results from all the studies, the team divided up the hypotheses in a number of ways before discarding certain ones. First, the team divided the hypotheses into those that addressed specific projects and those that addressed security cooperation in general. The team then divided the hypotheses into those that addressed the United States, the PN, or the relationship between the United States and the PN. Finally, the team identified hypotheses that contradicted one another.

The team decided not to include hypotheses that exclusively addressed a specific security cooperation project, because such results do not reflect differences in security cooperation effectiveness across countries (which is the focus of this effort); instead, selection process focused on *how* to implement security cooperation projects in an effective manner.

The team also decided to exclude hypotheses related to the provision of security cooperation assistance. Many studies focused on U.S. training and preparation for providing security cooperation support, or lessons learned or advice on how the United States could do a better job providing security cooperation support—for example, suggesting that the United States could improve its language and culture training, or that it could work harder to ensure unity of effort. We excluded these hypotheses not because they do not offer useful insights but because they are of little help in determining whether or not a potential partner is a good candidate for security cooperation.

There was a further interesting subset of hypotheses that we needed to consider: those that were partially or wholly contradictory. For example, many studies suggested that security cooperation was more likely to be effective with more capable partners, but at least one study argued that security cooperation is likely to be successful with *less* capable partners (because they have more room for improvement). Both hypotheses could be true. Another example of such a contradiction was in hypotheses regarding the role of third parties in providing assistance to partner countries. Some studies suggested that security cooperation is more likely to be successful if the United States works together with third parties; however, other studies suggested that the United States may not want to compete for influence in countries that already have a clear patron. Because these hypotheses depend on the specific situation or have multiple possible directions of influence, we decided not to include them in the propensity score portion of the tool, instead isolating them as "policy and strategy considerations," as described later in this chapter.

Synthesizing Related Hypotheses into Constructs and Categories

After sorting through the hypotheses to weed out those that were not useful for the tool or that were inappropriate for the core of the tool, approximately 70 hypotheses remained. Many of these remaining hypotheses were very similar to one another. Not surprisingly, the most common duplicative hypotheses related to the relationship between the United States and the PN. The overall idea is that security cooperation is more likely to be successful in partner countries that have a good long-term cooperative relationship with the United States that is based on shared interests and favorable perceptions. Many hypotheses also focused on the partner country's government—in particular, whether it was democratic.

The team combined similar hypotheses, creating unified theses that we refer to as *constructs*. The tool includes 27 constructs, which serve as its analytic core. Each construct has an associated weight, representing the strength of the contribution of that construct to propensity for effective security cooperation and the strength of the research contributing to that construct. (The weighting process is described in greater detail later in this chapter.) Although the literature led us to 27 distinct constructs that contribute to propensity of security cooperation effectiveness, we recognized that this was too many separate items for summary consideration by a policy audience. To facilitate consumption, we grouped the 27 constructs into ten categories. The ten categories provide a more succinct way to present information. Note that the categories do not reflect analytic importance and are just a summary convenience; all weights adhere to the constructs, not the categories. Table 3.2 lists each of the ten categories and the 27 constructs.

Table 3.2
Tool Categories and Constructs

CATEGORY 1: HISTORICAL QUALITY OF US SC/SFA/BPC PROVISION SC is more likely to be effective when the US provides an adequate amount of consistent SC funding to the PN
Construct 1.1: US SC/SFA/BPC funding consistent
Construct 1.2: US SC/SFA/BPC funding sufficient
CATEGORY 2: HISTORICAL TRACK RECORD OF SUCCESS WITH PN SC is more likely to be effective with a PN that has successfully implemented and sustained US or other foreign assistance in the past
Construct 2.1: US historical success with SC/BPC/SFA
Construct 2.2: Historical success with foreign aid
CATEGORY 3: US-PN RELATIONSHIP SC is more likely to be effective when the US and PN have a long-term relationship built on shared interests and a history of cooperation and where the US is viewed favorably by the PN
Construct 3.1: PN cooperation with US
Construct 3.2: PN citizen perception of US
Construct 3.3: Long-term relationship between US and PN
Construct 3.4: Shared interests between US and PN

Table 3.2—Continued

CATEGORY 4: SUPPORT FOR MILITARY IN/BY THE PN SC is more likely to be successful when the PN government and public support their military

Construct 4.1: PN government invests in military

Construct 4.2: PN public support for military

CATEGORY 5: ABSORPTIVE CAPACITY OF PN MILITARY SC is more likely to be successful when the PN military has sufficient capacity to absorb the SC being provided

Construct 5.1: PN military forces' absorptive capacity

Construct 5.2: PN absorptive capacity—technical

Construct 5.3: PN absorptive capacity—ministerial

CATEGORY 6: STRENGTH OF PN GOVERNMENT SC is more likely to be successful when the PN government has competent and strong institutions

Construct 6.1: PN government competence/strength

CATEGORY 7: PN GOVERNANCE SC is more likely to be successful with PNs that have good governments that are stable, not corrupt, and accountable to their people

Construct 7.1: PN democratic

Construct 7.2: PN government stability

Construct 7.3: PN government legitimacy

Construct 7.4: PN governance

Construct 7.5: Lack of PN government corruption

Construct 7.6: PN human rights record

CATEGORY 8: PN ECONOMIC STRENGTH SC is more likely to be effective with PNs with stable economies and a minimum level of economic development

Construct 8.1: PN economy

CATEGORY 9: PN SECURITY SITUATION SC is more likely to be successful in PNs without internal Instability or other serious security threats (though these may increase their need for SC)

Construct 9.1: PN security

CATEGORY 10: PRACTICAL EASE OF ENGAGING WITH PN SC is more likely to be successful with PNs that are easier to work with because they are small, speak English, have good infrastructure, and have signed all necessary agreements with the US

Construct 10.1: US-PN agreements—information sharing

Construct 10.2: US-PN agreements—legal status of US forces

Construct 10.3: US-PN common language

Construct 10.4: PN transportation infrastructure

Construct 10.5: PN communications Infrastructure

NOTE: SC = security cooperation.

Representation of Factors from the Prior Research in the Tool

The earlier RAND study, MG-1253/1-OSD, is both the inspiration for and the analytic core of the RAND Security Cooperation Prioritization and Propensity Matching Tool. While Table 3.2 lists all the constructs in the tool, Table 3.3 connects the constructs with their origins, listing the nine original key factors and the constructs that capture them, and then moving on to constructs that came entirely from other sources, as discussed in this chapter.

Policy and Strategy Considerations

As noted earlier, some of the hypotheses identified in the literature contradicted other hypotheses, or they were complicated and proposed multiple possible directions of impact on or rela-

Table 3.3
Index of Findings from the Prior Research with Constructs Developed Specifically for the Tool

Factors from *What Works Best When Building Partner Capacity and Under What Circumstances?* (MG-1253/1-OSD)	Constructs in the Tool
1. Spending more money on BPC or undertaking more BPC initiatives	**Construct 1.2:** US SC/SFA/BPC funding sufficient
2. Consistency in both funding and implementation of these initiatives	**Construct 1.1:** US SC/SFA/BPC funding consistent
3. Matching U.S. BPC efforts with PN objectives and absorptive capacity	Addressed in factors 6 and 9
4. Including a sustainment component in the initiatives	Not included; entirely within U.S. control
5. PN invests its own funds	**Construct 4.1:** PN government invests in military
6. PN has sufficient absorptive capacity	**Construct 5.1:** PN military forces' absorptive capacity **Construct 5.2:** PN absorptive capacity—technical **Construct 5.3:** PN absorptive capacity—ministerial
7. PN has high governance indicators	**Construct 6.1:** PN government competence/strength **Construct 7.1:** PN democratic **Construct 7.2:** PN government stability **Construct 7.3:** PN government legitimacy **Construct 7.4:** PN governance **Construct 7.5:** Lack of PN government corruption
8. PN has a strong economy	**Construct 8.1:** PN economy
9. PN shares broad security interests with the United States	**Construct 3.1:** PN cooperation with US **Construct 3.3:** Long-term relationship between US and PN **Construct 3.4:** Shared interests between US and PN **Construct 10.1:** US-PN agreements—information sharing **Construct 10.2:** US-PN agreements—legal status of US forces
Constructs added based on other studies, as described in Chapter Three	**Construct 2.1:** US historical success with SC/BPC/SFA **Construct 2.2:** Historical success with foreign aid **Construct 3.2:** PN citizen perception of US **Construct 4.2:** PN public support for military **Construct 7.6:** PN human rights record **Construct 9.1:** PN security situation **Construct 10.3:** US-PN common language **Construct 10.4:** PN transportation infrastructure **Construct 10.5:** PN communications Infrastructure

NOTE: SC = security cooperation.

tionships with propensity for security cooperation effectiveness. While we declined to include such hypotheses when distilling the constructs that contribute to the propensity score model, we recognized some of them as policy-relevant and as possible "red flags" that could and should affect security cooperation policy decisions. We include them in the tool in a separate area, unweighted and independent of the security cooperation propensity scores. These policy and strategic considerations provide tool users with additional information that may be relevant to decisions about resourcing and prioritization. The six policy and strategy considerations in the tool spreadsheets are listed in Table 3.4, along with the rationale for their inclusion or for their possible relevance.

Populating the Tool with Data

Each of the 27 constructs is represented by one or more measures or proxies. There are 66 measures in total (see Appendix A for a full list). For example, Construct 4.1, "PN government invests in military," is represented by multiple measures: a combination of total PN military spending per capita and total military budget as a percentage of gross domestic product (GDP). Construct 7.1, "PN democratic," is represented by a single measure, the Polity IV Democracy Index.

Each measure comes from an accessible database with global or nearly global coverage. The team used a variety of sources, from the World Bank, Stockholm International Peace Research Institute, Organisation for Economic Co-operation and Development, United Nations, Center for Systemic Peace, Gallup, and Jane's, as well as U.S. government agencies, including the U.S. Agency for International Development (USAID), the Bureau of Economic Analysis, and the Departments of State, Commerce, and Homeland Security. All data sources are listed at the end of this report and in the relevant tabs of the tool.

The measures are imperfect proxies for the constructs they represent. To address this unavoidable shortcoming, each measure was given a weight based on how closely it approximated the construct and how reliable and valid the data and data source were. For example, the

Table 3.4
Policy and Strategy Considerations

Policy and Strategy Considerations	Rationale
Largest allied contributor of foreign aid to PN (in millions of constant US $)	The United States could improve its chances for success by working with allies, or it may want to conserve money by not investing in a country where an ally is already engaged.
Total arms shipments from Russia or China to PN	It may or may not be worthwhile for the United States to compete for influence with a non-ally, depending on the country.
PN baseline military capability	On the one hand, low-capability PNs are attractive because there is room for improvement; on the other hand, high-baseline PNs are attractive because there is a high chance of success.
PN on State Department's list of state sponsors of terrorism	The United States does not support terrorism.
PN is a nuclear, biological, or chemical weapon proliferator	The United States does not support countries that proliferate weapons of mass destruction.
PN size index (population)	All other things being equal, smaller (in population, area, and military size) PNs cost less to assist but have less weight/mass with which to affect regional security.

absorptive capacity of a country's military, while very important, is also very difficult to measure. The team identified a dozen potential measures, but none was a particularly good proxy for the construct. On a scale of 0 to 1, where 1 would be assigned to a measure that perfectly represented the construct and 0 would indicate no representation whatsoever, the RAND team did not score any of these measures above 0.4. Other constructs, such as economic strength, are easier to measure. In that case, the team identified eight measures with proxy scores as high as 0.8. The next section describes the process used to weight constructs and measures and how they relate to lead to propensity scores in the tool.

Mathematical Approach to Measures, Constructs, and Categories and Their Weights

Building from the raw data up, the tool is essentially a collection of 66 measures that are grouped together and weighted to form 27 constructs. These constructs are then weighted based on the quality of evidence supporting the hypotheses they represent and the strength of the research contributing to that construct to create an overall propensity score. The 27 constructs are also grouped into summary categories, but these categories do not have weights assigned to them and do not directly connect to the overall propensity score for a country.

The measures come from the raw data sources listed at the end of this report and in the tool itself. Appendix D provides detailed instructions for updating the data to ensure the currency of the tool in future years. In some cases, more than one element of raw data will need to be combined to form a measure. For example, Measure 5.1.2, "PN military spending in millions constant US $ per troop," includes two data elements (military spending and number of troops) that combine to form a single measure. In other instances (most instances, in fact), the raw data and the measure are the same. After different data elements are combined as needed to form measures, the tool normalizes all measures to range from 0 to 1 across the countries for which data are available (as described in Appendix C). Where data are missing for a country, the weight for that measure is set to 0, so the missing datum does not contribute positively or negatively to the country's overall propensity score.

Where a construct is represented by only one measure, the country score for the measure and the country score for the construct will be the same. However, most constructs are represented by more than one measure. In this case, the measures are weighted and combined. The measure weights are derived from a subjective evaluation of how closely the measure approximates the construct. Many constructs are very difficult to measure—for example, the quality of the relationship between the United States and the partner nation. The weighted measures are combined (by weight) to make the overall construct score.

Construct weights are calculated based on five factors: (1) the overall proxy weight of the measures (our assessment of how well the measures represent the construct), (2) the strength of the correlation between the construct and the effectiveness of security cooperation, (3) the quality of the research supporting the construct, (4) the number of research studies supporting the construct, and (5) the extent to which the construct is duplicative or overlaps with other constructs. The second and third factors came out of the initial literature review (see Table 3.1 for an example), the fourth was recorded during the hypothesis-sifting process, and the first and fifth are based on the RAND team's holistic assessments.

Construct scores and weights combine to provide the overall propensity score for each country. The tool allows users to set their own construct weights, if desired. (See Chapter Four for a more detailed discussion.)

The ten category scores are also derived from the construct scores. We note, again, that the categories themselves are merely a means of displaying similar constructs in a manageable format and have no inherent weights themselves. (That is, they simply report the underlying weight accruing to the constructs they summarize.) Additional detail on the mathematical approach to the tool is included in Appendix C.

Validation of the Tool

In an effort to validate our prior assumptions based on the available data, we sought to compare results from the tool against the detailed case studies compiled as part of the earlier RAND study. The project team members who worked on MG-1253/1-OSD were asked to score the 27 constructs used here for each of the 29 case-study countries. For each of the constructs, the analysts were asked to score the country as low (0.17), low/medium (0.33), medium (0.5), medium/high (0.66), or high (0.83). These expert assessments were then compared with the construct scores generated by the tool based on the weighted proxy measures, all of which are normed to fall between 0 and 1 and thus should fall relatively near the low/medium/high bands generated by the holistic expert scoring.

Constructs with an average absolute variation of less than 0.17 were considered good, as that indicated agreement or consonance within an approximate band. For example, if an individual case was scored as low on a construct, the 0.17 that represents "low" would match scores in the tool ranging from 0 to 0.34, all of which are in the "low" approximate band. Constructs with average variation between 0.17 and 0.34 were considered moderate, as such constructs were, on average, about one "band" off. Constructs with average variation greater than 0.33 were considered poor or concerning. Fortunately, none of the constructs had an average absolute variation greater than 0.33. We also tallied the number of single-case instances in which the holistic expert score differed from the tool-generated score by 0.33 or more for each construct. Full details are reported in Appendix B.

All constructs for which proxy measures produced moderate levels of concordance and/or that had a relatively high incidence of individual case deviations were those for which we had already recognized that the measures used were suboptimal proxies for the constructs yet were the best we could find. Proxy weights for these (thankfully few) measures were further reduced based on this validation effort.

The RAND Security Cooperation Prioritization and Propensity Matching Tool

This chapter describes the tool, details its layout and function, and provides some summary information about its use.

Description of the Tool

The RAND Security Cooperation Prioritization and Propensity Matching Tool is a Microsoft Excel workbook with 17 nested worksheet tabs (described in Table 4.1). The first spreadsheet tab ("Read Me") provides an overview of the tool and some instructions for its use, should a user receive the tool without this document. The next three sheets ("Top Sheet," "Subordinate Constructs," and "Measures") display the overall propensity scores, category scores, construct scores, and measures for each of the 195 countries or PNs. These three sheets also present the important strategy and policy considerations, along with other information, including user-provided PN priority, fiscal year (FY) 2010 (or user-updated) U.S. security cooperation funding levels for that country, and calculated funding per PN troop. The next twelve spreadsheet tabs include the raw data inputted from publicly accessible global data sources, which can be updated by the user. The final tab ("Category Construct Weights") provides the default weights for each category and construct in the tool and offers the user the opportunity to adjust these weights. The remainder of this chapter describes the results, weighting, and data input spreadsheets in detail.

Viewing the Results

The top-level sheet ("Top Sheet") includes, from left to right, the country, its International Organization for Standardization (ISO) and Federal Information Processing Standard (FIPS) codes, the geographic combatant command (COCOM) in which it is located, the overall propensity score for that partner (raw score and "stoplight" color-coded score), the user-provided priority for that partner, FY 2010 total U.S. security cooperation expenditures for the partner, spending per troop, propensity score contributions from each of the ten categories, and the six policy and strategy considerations (see Figure 4.1). The "Top Sheet" also includes a sorter box in the upper left corner that allows a user to sort the data, ascending or descending, by country, COCOM, overall score, priority, expenditures, spend per troop, or any of the ten summary categories. Sorting on the top sheet affects all three of the top sheets (down through "Measures").

Table 4.1
Spreadsheets in the Tool

	Spreadsheet Name	Description
	Read Me	Describes the tool and provides information on how to use and update it
Results	Top Sheet	Main summary of results, including both overall summary propensity score and category scores. Also included: priority rank, security cooperation expenditures (total and per troop), and strategy and policy considerations
	Subordinate Constructs	"Top Sheet" plus construct scores
	Measures	"Top Sheet" plus construct and measure scores
Data Input	Data Tables	Repository for data sources used to compute measures in across multiple categories
	CAT 1 Data & Measure Weights ... CAT 10 Data & Measure Weights	Data sources and measures divided by category; there are ten separate spreadsheets, each with information on data sources as well as the actual data tables
	Strategy & Policy Considerations	Similar to the "Data Measures & Weights" tabs for the ten categories; contains information and data sources used to compute the strategy and policy considerations
Weights	Category Construct Weights	Allows the user to adjust the weight of each of the constructs and categories; RAND has set default weights

NOTE: Security cooperation expenditures are based on "military assistance" as reported in the USAID *Greenbook*. This includes the following accounts: Foreign Military Sales, Afghan Security Forces Fund, Drug Interdiction and Counter-Drug Activities, Excess Defense Articles, Foreign Military Financing, Former Soviet Union Threat Reduction, International Military Education and Training, Iraq Security Forces Fund, Pakistan Counterinsurgency Fund, and Peacekeeping Operations. "Military assistance" does not include other forms of assistance provided by DoD, such as Overseas Humanitarian, Disaster, and Civic Aid, the Defense Health Program, and activities supported by Operations and Maintenance funds.

Nested sheets provide ever-increasing granularity, with the second layer ("Subordinate Constructs") showing the 27 constructs that directly inform the overall propensity score, and the third layer ("Measures") displaying the individual measures/proxies informing the constructs. Note that the "Measures" tab is where a user would input user-assigned priorities and is the first tab on which the user can directly make changes to the content of the tool. (Higher tabs and many spaces on the tabs are "locked" to prevent unintended changes to the tool's content.)

Sheets below "Measures" include space, and accompanying instructions, for future users who wish to update the currency of the data informing the tool in future years. Further instructions are provided in Appendix D. The final spreadsheet tab, "Category Construct Weights" is where a user could impose his or her own weights on the tool, either to test a different hypothesis or to focus on specific constructs at the expense of others. The use of this tab is discussed in the next section.

Figure 4.1
Screenshot of the "Top Sheet" Spreadsheet

Sort by

Sort by	
Country	◄ ►
COCOM	◄ ►
Overall Score	◄ ►
Priority	◄ ►
SC/SFA/BPC Expenditures	◄ ►
SC/SFA/BPC Expenditures by PN Troop	◄ ►
Category #1	◄ ►
Category #2	◄ ►
Category #3	◄ ►
Category #4	◄ ►
Category #5	◄ ►
Category #6	◄ ►
Category #7	◄ ►
Category #8	
Category #9	
Category #10	

Column legend:
- OVERALL SUMMARY PROPENSITY SCORE — Weighted average of CAT 1–CAT 10
- TOTAL SC/SFA/BPC EXPENDITURES ($$$) — FY10 US Expenditures ($M) for security cooperation with PN
- TOTAL SC/SFA/BPC EXPENDITURES PER PN TROOP ($$$)
- CAT 1: HISTORICAL QUALITY OF US SC/SFA/BPC PROVISION
- CAT 2: HISTORICAL TRACK RECORD OF SUCCESS WITH PN
- CAT 3: US-PN RELATIONSHIP
- CAT 4: SUPPORT FOR MILITARY IN/BY THE PN
- CAT 5: ABSORPTIVE CAPACITY OF PN MILITARY
- CAT 6: STRENGTH OF THE PN GOVERNMENT
- CAT 7: PN GOVERNANCE
- CAT 8: PN ECONOMIC STRENGTH
- CAT 9: PN SECURITY SITUATION
- CAT 10: PRACTICAL EASE OF ENGAGING WITH PN
- Strategic/Policy Considerations: Largest allied contributor of foreign aid; Percentage of total arms shipments that is from China or Russia; Efficacy of security forces (1 = low, 2 = medium, 3 = high); PN on the State Department list of state sponsors of terrorism; NBC weapons proliferator; PN size index (population)

#	Country or Territory	ISO	FIPS	COCOM	OVERALL	PRIORITY	TOTAL EXP $$$	PER TROOP $$$	CAT 1	CAT 2	CAT 3	CAT 4	CAT 5	CAT 6	CAT 7	CAT 8	CAT 9	CAT 10	Largest allied	% China/Russia	Efficacy	State sponsor	NBC	PN size
1	Afghanistan	AFG	AF	CENTCOM	0.36	X	30,265.4	22,663	0.76	0.08	0.32	0.73	0.22	0.11	0.23	0.20	0.23	0.16	USA	14	1	0	0	0.77
2	Albania	ALB	AL	EUCOM	0.56	X	5.1	353	0.39	0.57	0.68	0.44	0.58	0.52	0.65	0.61	0.69	0.40	ITA	0	2	0	0	0.35
3	Algeria	DZA	AG	AFRICOM	0.45	X	1.0	3	0.51	0.79	0.22	0.73	0.52	0.27	0.26	0.45	0.49	0.22	FRA	85	2	0	0	0.77
4	Andorra	ADO	AN	EUCOM	0.75	X	0.0				0.67	0.77	0.89	0.90	0.74	0.68	0.94	0.47		0	3	0	0	0.10
5	Angola	AGO	AO	AFRICOM	0.43	X	0.4	3	0.60		0.42		0.39	0.19	0.32	0.16	0.47	0.16	USA	0	2	0	0	0.70
6	Antigua and Barbuda	ATG	AC	SOUTHCOM	0.56	X	0.4	12,941	0.15	0.59	0.54	0.25	0.55	0.74	0.72	0.70	0.67	0.79	JPN	50	2	0	0	0.11
7	Argentina	ARG	AR	SOUTHCOM	0.52	X	0.7	14	0.42	0.78	0.57	0.67	0.66	0.42	0.63	0.62	0.65	0.43	JPN	50	2	0	0	0.78
8	Armenia	ARM	AM	EUCOM	0.50	X	3.4	65	0.50	0.69	0.30	0.67	0.46	0.55	0.49	0.52	0.42	0.42	USA	47	2	0	0	0.35
9	Australia	AUS	AS	PACOM	0.84	X	0.0	0			0.80	0.71	0.94	0.95	0.95	0.89	0.88	0.75		0	3	0	0	0.74
10	Austria	AUT	AU	EUCOM	0.78	X	0.0				0.71	0.37	0.91	0.92	0.95	0.88	0.94	0.65		0	2	0	0	0.53
11	Azerbaijan	AZE	AJ	EUCOM	0.46	X	3.9	50	0.65	0.48	0.34	0.73	0.37	0.29	0.19	0.62	0.36	0.48	USA	80	2	0	0	0.54
12	Bahamas	BHS	BF	NORTHCOM	0.67	X	5.2	8,140	0.47	0.63	0.64		0.62	0.76	0.83	0.78	0.71	0.72		0	2	0	0	0.17
13	Bahrain	BHR	BA	CENTCOM	0.52	X	15.9	1,053	0.37	0.50	0.36	0.69	0.51	0.74	0.45	0.73	0.61	0.57		0	2	0	0	0.23
14	Bangladesh	BGD	BG	PACOM	0.35	X	4.0	12	0.36	0.46	0.44	0.56	0.32	0.26	0.37	0.28	0.43	0.16	GBR	66	2	0	0	0.86
15	Barbados	BRB	BB	SOUTHCOM	0.74	X	0.5	1,148	1.00	0.68	0.57		0.64	0.83	0.88	0.74	0.72	0.77	JPN	0	2	0	0	0.16
16	Belarus	BLR	BO	EUCOM	0.38	X	0.0	0			0.21	0.43	0.36	0.20	0.29	0.75	0.48	0.51	USA	50	2	0	0	0.55
17	Belgium	BEL	BE	EUCOM	0.73	X	0.0	0		0.92	0.67	0.42	0.83	0.90	0.72	0.86	0.93	0.67	USA	0	3	0	0	0.58
18	Belize	BLZ	BH	SOUTHCOM	0.41	X	13.5	5,048	0.34	0.52	0.42	0.23	0.52	0.41	0.46	0.39	0.39	0.50	JPN	0	2	0	0	0.17
19	Benin	BEN	BN	AFRICOM	0.37	X	0.5	41	0.26	0.32	0.53	0.23	0.52	0.38	0.55	0.23	0.46	0.18	USA	0	2	0	0	0.54
20	Bhutan	BTN	BT	PACOM	0.46	X	0.0			0.33	0.40		0.47	0.56	0.55	0.40	0.59	0.23	JPN	0	2	0	0	0.21
21	Bolivia	BOL	BL	SOUTHCOM	0.37	X	0.3	11	0.13	0.36	0.38	0.48	0.38	0.32	0.43	0.45	0.50	0.24	USA	40	2	0	0	0.56
22	Bosnia and Herzegovina	BIH	BK	EUCOM	0.46	X	5.5	501	0.62	0.57	0.44	0.31	0.32	0.40	0.33	0.59	0.44	0.46	AUT	0	1	0	0	0.38
23	Botswana	BWA	BC	AFRICOM	0.59	X	1.1	95	0.6-	0.49	0.53	0.59	0.64	0.73	0.75	0.42	0.80	0.52	USA	0	2	0	0	0.27

RAND TL112-4.1

Implementing User-Selected Weights

In addition to the range of data sheets, the tool includes a tab that displays the weight applied to each construct and allows the user to apply user specified weights. This is the "Category Construct Weights" tab, the last tab in the tool. As discussed, the RAND team has set default weights, based on five factors:

1. extent to which measures are effective proxies for the construct
2. strength of the correlation or association between the construct and the effectiveness of security cooperation
3. quality of the research supporting the construct
4. number of research studies supporting the construct
5. extent to which the construct is duplicative with other constructs.

The values for four of those weights are displayed on the "Category Construct Weights" tab; the first weight, the proxy weight, is captured in the category data tabs (e.g., "CAT 1 Data & Measure Weights"). Below the RAND default weights, the user has the option of inputting his or her own weights for the categories and constructs. The user does not need to input category weights; they will be derived automatically from the construct weights. Although the user can input category weights if desired, the RAND team would discourage this because the categories are used only to group the constructs and makes the results easier to display and understand quickly (and are not meaningful in and of themselves); only the construct weights are aggregated to produce the final propensity score.

Updating the Tool as New Data Become Available

The tool is designed to be reusable and updated by a generalist user (i.e., someone who understands basic Excel) without the assistance of RAND authors/analysts. To this end, the team sought data sources for the measures that were publicly available and would be updated regularly.[1] The "Read Me" spreadsheet includes instructions for inputting new data. Additional instructions are included in Appendix D.

---

[1] The baseline data in the spreadsheet are from a wide variety of publicly accessible sources. It is possible that some of these data sources will no longer be available or that they will no longer provide a particular type of data needed for the tool. If no equivalent data are available to update the tool, the user can choose to keep the original figure or leave the measure blank, and the tool will adjust by giving greater weight to the remaining data in the construct.

CHAPTER FIVE

Conclusions: Appropriate Employment of the Tool

The RAND Security Cooperation Prioritization and Propensity Matching Tool is a preliminary diagnostic device that has the virtues of being systematic, based on global data, and treating every country the same without allowing personality or expertise to play a role. It is *not* a substitute for thoughtful consideration of the nuances of individual countries, nor is it meant to directly support decisions in the absence of that nuanced and thoughtful consideration. What it *is* ideal for is identifying a relatively small number of countries to scrutinize further and discerning whether possible mismatches are actual mismatches, leading to possibly fruitful policy discussion. Further, the tool will clearly expose which individual constructs have been scored as wanting in a given country, helping to focus country-level inquiry when greater nuance is sought.

Using the Tool: An Example

There is no single right way to use the tool. However, the natural place to start is with the overall propensity scores. Has the United States given security cooperation funding to countries with a low probability of success? The answer is yes. Figure 5.1 shows countries ranked by their propensity scores, from lowest to highest. Many countries with low propensity scores did not receive U.S. security cooperation funding in FY 2011 (e.g., North Korea, Zimbabwe). However, many other countries with low propensity scores did receive U.S. security cooperation funding in FY 2011, and sometimes in rather large amounts.

It is important to point out that the tool does not answer the question, "*Should* the United States give security cooperation funding to countries where there is a low probability of success?" One factor not included in this list is the priority ranking of countries based on U.S. strategic interests.[1] An ongoing conundrum for policymakers is that the reason a country is not a good candidate for U.S. assistance is sometimes also what makes it a priority. As noted in the 2010 *Quadrennial Defense Review Report*, "Threats to our security in the decades to come are more likely to emanate from state weakness than from state strength."[2]

Somalia and Yemen illustrate this case. Both are weak states with little control over their territory, and they thus provide safe havens for terrorists and other actors that threaten U.S. interests. In these cases, there is probably good reason for the United States to provide some sort of assistance. Other countries may be important for different reasons: the need to move

---

[1] It is up to the user to input the priority ranking of countries. This ranking will likely be based on classified documents.

[2] U.S. Department of Defense, 2010.

Figure 5.1
Screenshot of Countries Sorted by Overall Propensity Score (Ascending)

							Overall	Priority	$$$	$$$
Sort by							OVERALL SUMMARY PROPENSITY SCORE Weighted average of CAT 1–CAT 10	PRIORITY/PRIORITY RANK	TOTAL SC/SFA/BPC EXPENDITURES FY10 US Expenditures ($M) for security cooperation with PN	TOTAL SC/SFA/BPC EXPENDITURES PER PN TROOP
Country	▲ ▼	Category #1	▲ ▼							
COCOM	▲ ▼	Category #2	▲ ▼							
Overall Score	▲ ▼	Category #3	▲ ▼							
Priority	▲ ▼	Category #4	▲ ▼							
SC/SFA/BPC Expenditures	▲ ▼	Category #5	▲ ▼							
SC/SFA/BPC Expenditures by PN Troop	▲ ▼	Category #6	▲ ▼							
		Category #7	▲ ▼							
		Category #8	▲ ▼							
		Category #9	▲ ▼							
		Category #10	▲ ▼							
#	**Country or Territory**		**ISO**	**FIPS**	**COCOM**					
160	Somalia		SOM	SO	AFRICOM		0.12	X	75.3	52,000
89	Korea (North), Democratic People's Repub		PRK	KN	PACOM		0.16	X	0.0	0
55	Eritrea		ERI	ER	AFRICOM		0.22	X	0.0	0
69	Guinea		GIN	GV	AFRICOM		0.22	X	0.0	83
133	Palestinian Authority (Palestinian Territorie		WBG	0	CENTCOM		0.23	X	0.0	
195	Zimbabwe		ZWE	ZI	AFRICOM		0.24	X	0.0	
165	Sudan		SDN	SU	AFRICOM		0.24	X	0.0	442
54	Equatorial Guinea		GNQ	EK	AFRICOM		0.24	X	0.0	
181	Turkmenistan		TKM	TX	CENTCOM		0.25	X	3.3	482
104	Madagascar		MDG	MA	AFRICOM		0.26	X	0.0	0
34	Chad		TCD	CD	AFRICOM		0.26	X	0.8	26
70	Guinea-Bissau		GNB	PU	AFRICOM		0.27	X	0.0	0
127	Niger		NER	NG	AFRICOM		0.27	X	0.1	0
172	Tajikistan		TJK	TI	CENTCOM		0.27	X	8.3	1,037
72	Haiti		HTI	HA	SOUTHCOM		0.27	X	1.9	
94	Lao People's Democratic Republic		LAO	LA	PACOM		0.28	X	0.2	1
121	Myanmar (Burma)		MMR	BM	PACOM		0.29	X	0.0	0
38	Comoros		COM	CN	AFRICOM		0.29	X	0.2	
111	Mauritania		MRT	MR	AFRICOM		0.29	X	1.4	19
193	Yemen		YEM	YM	CENTCOM		0.30	X	21.1	101
120	Mozambique		MOZ	MZ	AFRICOM		0.30	X	1.7	45
39	Congo (Brazzaville)/ Republic of Congo		COG	CF	AFRICOM		0.30	X	0.1	8
57	Ethiopia		ETH	ET	AFRICOM		0.30	X	0.7	2
150	Sao Tome and Principe		STP	TP	AFRICOM		0.32	X	0.3	
123	Nepal		NPL	NP	PACOM		0.32	X	1.9	11
40	Congo (Kinshasa)/ Democratic Republic of		ZAR	CG	AFRICOM		0.32	X	22.0	103
176	Togo		TGO	TO	AFRICOM		0.32	X	0.7	22
44	Cuba		CUB	CU	SOUTHCOM		0.33	X	0.0	

RAND *TL112-5.1*

troops and equipment to and from Afghanistan, recent or ongoing humanitarian disasters, proximity to the United States, preventing illicit trafficking, and so on. For example, peace-keeping operations related to implementation of the Comprehensive Peace Agreement and the ongoing Darfur crisis are likely the main drivers of military assistance to Sudan and Chad.[3]

---

[3] Total SC/BPC/SFA expenditures include peacekeeping operations funds, which are accounted for by the location of the operation they support rather than the country or organization that received the funds (like most other accounts). What

High-priority countries tend to get more funding and attention. Previous research shows that adequate and consistent U.S. security cooperation can contribute to success.[4] However, for countries on the very bottom of the propensity score ranking, the risk of failure is still very high. U.S. security cooperation with these countries should explicitly take this into account. For instance, the need to build the capacity of PN troops to fight terrorists should be balanced against the risk that those same troops will participate in a coup or become terrorists themselves (in the near or long term).

It is likely that some of the countries in Figure 5.1 are low-priority countries. The question in these cases is whether *any* U.S. security cooperation is warranted. Lower-priority countries tend to get smaller amounts of funding. There may be cases in which the U.S. military can achieve limited goals with limited funds. However, given the high risk of failure, it is still worth asking whether scarce U.S. security cooperation funding should instead be focused on higher-priority countries with a greater chance of success. When time is not of the essence, it might be useful to work with the U.S. Department of State to help build the foundation for future security cooperation funding.

The tool is useful for highlighting high-risk countries, both low- and high-priority. However, prior to making a recommendation about modifying security cooperation plans for any particular country, additional research would be needed. The tool is potentially very useful for helping to identify cases for further scrutiny, but we openly and candidly acknowledge that it does not capture country-specific nuances that could affect propensity for security cooperation effectiveness or practical prioritization. The tool would be ideal for prioritizing efforts to investigate country details when it would be impossible to conduct a detailed review of every country with which the United States has a security cooperation relationship—for instance, during the program and budget review.

Other Uses for the Tool

One possible application of the tool is the one for which it was intended: identifying mismatches between propensity for security cooperation and current funding levels, and conducting detailed country-specific analyses of those mismatches. The results of the detailed analyses would then inform recommendations for adjusting future security cooperation funding in those countries. Such research could be done directly in support of one of the cyclical planning processes, such as the program and budget review process overseen by the Office of the Secretary of Defense.

Another application would be to conduct "excursions" or "thought experiments," looking at specific cases, making changes to the underlying data or assumptions to see what changes, and creating and exploring "what if?" scenarios (e.g., "What if construct X were improved in country Y?"). This might be particularly useful when a country of interest is a high national security priority but a low security cooperation propensity partner, particularly for identifying what other kinds of development, support, or policy change might improve propensity and by how much.

---

this means is that it's likely the peacekeeping funds listed under Sudan did not go to the government of Sudan but to the countries and organizations contributing military forces to the peacekeeping operation in Sudan.

[4]   Paul et al., 2013.

Cautions

As noted, the tool provides a starting point for asking sometimes-hard questions about the relationship between U.S. security cooperation funding, U.S. priorities, and the likelihood of success in specific countries. However, it is not a substitute for strategic thought. There is no one-size-fits-all automated approach to choosing one set of countries that should get funding and another set that should not. The purpose of the tool is to highlight potential mismatches for further study and, perhaps, to highlight areas of concern to be addressed as part of that inquiry. In the remainder of this section, we outline two further cautions to keep in mind when using the tool.

Global Quantitative Data Lack Contextual Nuance

Digging into the tool's underlying data can help add detail, but the global quantitative measures used in the tool lack nuance. For instance, the tool can point to a rocky relationship between the United States and a PN, but it cannot identify the key disagreements, their depth, or their potential for resolution. It can indicate governance issues, but it cannot explain their source. Most importantly, the tool cannot tell you what, exactly, the United States wants to achieve in a given country and why.

The Analysis Underlying the Constructs Varies in Quality

Not all of the constructs in the tool are validated by empirical analysis. The vast majority of the research on security cooperation is based on case studies and personal experience. The tool is built on the foundation of empirical research conducted for the RAND report *What Works Best When Building Partner Capacity and Under What Circumstances?* (MG-1252/1-OSD).[5] However, it is important to note that even this research was based on only 29 case studies. That is a larger body of evidence than that of many other studies, but it is still not nearly global. The foundation of the model is, in Bayesian terms, "all prior."

Suggestions for Further Research

The tool itself could be further refined in a number of ways. If the underlying model for the tool is, in effect, a Bayesian prior based on received wisdom and existing research, the model could be refined by examining the observed posterior distribution—that is, the observed correlation between prognosticated propensity scores and actual security cooperation outcomes. This would be easier to do if DoD's plans to standardize security cooperation effectiveness measures bear fruit, because outcome data would then be easier to identify and collect.

Another way to improve the tool would be to do additional research on constructs related to security cooperation effectiveness. Using case-study methods similar to those used for MG-1253/1-OSD, further research could examine more cases with the expressed intent of examining which constructs are most (or least) important in determining security cooperation outcomes, further refining the constructs and their weights.

---

[5] Paul et al., 2013.

Another possible refinement would, in fact, be more of a redoing: to calibrate the tool to pursue specific security cooperation goals rather than generic security cooperation goals, such as BPC for counterterrorism or building PN maritime forces.

Finally, the tool could be improved through sensitivity analyses examining how changes in data, changes in data quality, or changes in construct weights would affect the model. Such an effort could lead to an ability to calculate uncertainty for the propensity scores offered, something the current tool does not offer.

Important technical note: The tool is a macro-enabled Excel worksheet. If macros are not enabled, many important functions (such as sorting) will not work.

Categories, Constructs, and Measures

Table A.1 provides the full list of categories, constructs, and measures in the tool, along with data sources. More detailed information on the sources cited here can be found in the "Data Sources" section at the end of this report and in the relevant tabs of the tool.

Table A.1
Full List of Categories, Constructs, and Measures

CATEGORY 1: HISTORICAL QUALITY OF US SC/SFA/BPC PROVISION
SC is more likely to be effective when the US provides an adequate amount of consistent SC funding to the PN

Construct 1.1: US SC/SFA/BPC funding consistent

  Measure 1.1.1: Normalized sum of annual decreases in US SC/SFA/BPC funding below median during 5-year span (Source: USAID *Greenbook*)

Construct 1.2: US SC/SFA/BPC funding sufficient

  Measure 1.2.1: US SC/SFA/BPC funding plus PN military spending per PN troop (average over 5-year span) (Sources: USAID *Greenbook*, SIPRI Military Expenditure Database, World Bank World Development Indicators)

CATEGORY 2: HISTORICAL TRACK RECORD OF SUCCESS WITH PN
SC is more likely to be effective with a PN that has successfully implemented and sustained US or other foreign assistance in the past

---

Construct 2.1: US historical success with SC/BPC/SFA

  Measure 2.1.1: Lag correlation between US SC/SFA/BPC funding and PN military expenditure (Sources: USAID *Greenbook* and SIPRI)

  Measure 2.1.2: Lag correlation between US SC/SFA/BPC funding and PN military sophistication (Sources: USAID *Greenbook* and Global Peace Index)

  Measure 2.1.3: Lag correlation between US SC/SFA/BPC funding and PN security force efficacy (Sources: USAID *Greenbook* and Jane's)

Construct 2.2: Historical success with foreign aid

  Measure 2.2.1: Lag correlation between all foreign aid to PN and PN HDI (Sources: OECD and UNDP)

CATEGORY 3: US-PN RELATIONSHIP
SC is more likely to be effective when the US and PN have a long-term relationship built on shared interests and a history of cooperation and where the US is viewed favorably by the PN

Construct 3.1: PN cooperation with US

  Measure 3.1.1: PN troop contributions per capita (millions) to coalition operations, last 10 years (Sources: Georgetown University, United Nations Department of Peacekeeping Operations, and World Bank)

  Measure 3.1.2: PN involvement with multilateral institutions (Source: Jane's)

Construct 3.2: PN citizen perception of US

  Measure 3.2.1: Percentage of PN population that approves of US leadership (Source: Gallup)

  Measure 3.2.2: US-PN travel (ratio of US total travel and PN size) (Source: U.S. Department of Commerce, International Trade Administration)

  Measure 3.2.3: Nonimmigrant admissions to the US per capita (Source: U.S. Department of Homeland Security)

Construct 3.3: Long-term relationship between US and PN

  Measure 3.3.1: US Foreign Direct Investment (FDI) flows (E + 1) to PN as a % of PN GDP (Source: U.S. Bureau of Economic Analysis)

  Measure 3.3.2: Trade between US and PN as a % of PN GDP (Source: U.S. Department of Commerce, Foreign Trade Division)

Table A.1—Continued

CATEGORY 3: US-PN RELATIONSHIP (cont.)
SC is more likely to be effective when the US and PN have a long-term relationship built on shared interests and a history of cooperation and where the US is viewed favorably by the PN

> **Measure 3.3.3:** Sum of PN university exchange students in US and US university exchange students in PN per PN capita (Source: Institute of International Education)

> **Measure 3.3.4:** Treaties with the US: defense, nonaggression, and visa (Sources: U.S. Department of State, Bureau of Consular Affairs, and Leeds et al., 2002)

Construct 3.4: Shared interests between US and PN

> **Measure 3.4.1:** Voting coincidence w/US (previous two years), UN General Assembly important resolutions and consensus actions (Source: U.S. Department of State, Bureau of International Organizations)

CATEGORY 4: SUPPORT FOR MILITARY IN/BY THE PN
SC is more likely to be successful when the PN government and public support their military

Construct 4.1: PN government invests in military

> **Measure 4.1.1:** Total military expenditure in millions constant US $

> **Measure 4.1.2:** PN military budget as % of GDP

Construct 4.2: PN public support for military

> **Measure 4.2.1:** Pew/World Values polling data

CATEGORY 5: ABSORPTIVE CAPACITY OF PN MILITARY
SC is more likely to be successful when the PN military has sufficient capacity to absorb the SC being provided

Construct 5.1: PN military forces' absorptive capacity

> **Measure 5.1.1:** PN military sophistication (Source: Global Peace Index)

> **Measure 5.1.2:** PN military spending in millions constant US $ per troop

> **Measure 5.1.3:** Efficacy of security forces (Source: Jane's)

Construct 5.2: PN absorptive capacity—technical

> **Measure 5.2.1:** US patents granted annually to PN residents per capita

> **Measure 5.2.2:** Royalty and license fees/payments per GDP

> **Measure 5.2.3:** Secondary enrollment ratio (% gross)

> **Measure 5.2.4:** Adult literacy rate

> **Measure 5.2.5:** Tertiary enrollment ratio (% gross)

Construct 5.3: PN absorptive capacity—ministerial

> **Measure 5.3.1:** WGI Government Effectiveness rating

> **Measure 5.3.2:** GDP per capita growth, average over last 5 years

> **Measure 5.3.3:** State control of security forces

> **Measure 5.3.4:** Professionalism of security forces

Table A.1—Continued

CATEGORY 6: STRENGTH OF PN GOVERNMENT SC is more likely to be successful when the PN government has competent and strong institutions

Construct 6.1: PN government competency/strength

    Measure 6.1.1: WGI Government Effectiveness Index

    Measure 6.1.2: WGI Regulatory Quality Index

    Measure 6.1.3: WGI Rule of Law Index

CATEGORY 7: PN GOVERNANCE SC is more likely to be successful with PNs that have good governments that are stable, not corrupt, and accountable to their people

Construct 7.1: PN democratic

    Measure 7.1.1: Polity IV Project Democracy Index

Construct 7.2: PN government stability

    Measure 7.2.1: Political Stability/No Violence Index (Source: World Bank)

Construct 7.3: PN government legitimacy

    Measure 7.3.1: Legitimacy sub-index of the State Fragility Index

Construct 7.4: PN governance

    Measure 7.4.1: Government Effectiveness Index (Source: World Bank)

Construct 7.5: Lack of PN government corruption

    Measure 7.5.1: Transparency International Corruption Perceptions Index

Construct 7.6: PN human rights record

    Measure 7.6.1: Political Terror Scale (Source: Amnesty International)

    Measure 7.6.2: Political Terror Scale (Source: U.S. Department of State via Amnesty International)

CATEGORY 8: PN ECONOMIC STRENGTH SC is more likely to be effective with PNs with stable economies and a minimum level of economic development

Construct 8.1: PN economy

    Measure 8.1.1: Percentage of population in poverty

    Measure 8.1.2: Multidimensional Poverty Index

    Measure 8.1.3: Percentage of population living on less than $1.25 (US) per day

    Measure 8.1.4: Human Development Index (HDI)

    Measure 8.1.5: Gender Gap Index

    Measure 8.1.6: GDP per capita (PPP)

    Measure 8.1.7: Economy sub-index of Legatum Prosperity Index

    Measure 8.1.8: Global Competitiveness Index

Table A.1—Continued

CATEGORY 9: PN SECURITY SITUATION
SC is more likely to be successful in PNs without internal instability or other serious security threats (though these may increase their need for SC)

Construct 9.1: PN security

    Measure 9.1.1: Number of external and internal conflicts fought

    Measure 9.1.2: Level of organized conflict (internal)

    Measure 9.1.3: Likelihood of violent demonstrations

    Measure 9.1.4: Relations with neighboring countries

    Measure 9.1.5: Major episodes of political violence

    Measure 9.1.6: Internal Security Stability Rating (Source: Jane's)

    Measure 9.1.7: External Security Stability Rating (Source: Jane's)

CATEGORY 10: PRACTICAL EASE OF ENGAGING WITH PN
SC is more likely to be successful with PNs that are easier to work with because they are small, speak English, have good infrastructure, and have signed all necessary agreements with the US

Construct 10.1: US-PN agreements—information sharing

    Measure 10.1.1: No proxy measure identified

Construct 10.2: US-PN agreements—legal status of US forces

    Measure 10.2.1: PN status of forces (SOFA) agreements with the US

Construct 10.3: US-PN common language

    Measure 10.3.1: English is an official language (yes/no)

Construct 10.4: PN transportation infrastructure

    Measure 10.4.1: Railways, goods transported (million ton-km) per 100K people

    Measure 10.4.2: Quality of port infrastructure

    Measure 10.4.3: Air transport, freight (million ton-km) per 100K people

    Measure 10.4.4: Number of C-130/C-17–compatible runways

Construct 10.5: PN communications infrastructure

    Measure 10.5.1: Telephone lines per 100 people

    Measure 10.5.2: Cell phone subscriptions per 100 people

    Measure 10.5.3: Internet users per 100 people

NOTE: HDI = Human Development Index. OECD = Organisation for Economic Co-operation and Development. PPP = purchasing power parity. SC = security cooperation. SIPRI = Stockholm International Peace Research Institute. UNDP = United Nations Development Programme. WGI = Worldwide Governance Indicators.

Tool Validation Through Case Studies

To validate the proxy measures used in the RAND Security Cooperation Prioritization and Propensity Matching Tool, we conducted a separate analysis of the tool constructs for the 29 countries that were included as case studies in a previous RAND report, *What Works Best When Building Partner Capacity and Under What Circumstances?* (MG-1253/1-OSD).[1] In this analysis, we compared expert assessments derived from detailed knowledge of the specific cases with the assessments made by the tool using nuance-free global data to see how closely the scores generated by the tool matched the more informed subjective assessments.

Project team members who worked on the earlier study were asked to score 24 of the constructs used in the tool for each of the 29 case-study countries based on their holistic knowledge of and familiarity with those cases rather than the selected proxy measures.[2] The constructs were scored categorically for each case-study country as low, low/medium, medium, medium/high, or high. Normed quantitative values were assigned to each category as follows: low (0.17), low/medium (0.33), medium (0.5), medium/high (0.66), or high (0.83). These expert assessments were then compared with the construct scores generated by the tool based on the weighted proxy measures (all of which have been normed to scale between 0 and 1). The absolute value of the difference between the two scores was calculated to determine the degree of variation or discrepancy between the two scores.

Constructs with an average absolute variation of less than 0.17 were considered good, those with average variation between 0.17 and 0.33 were considered moderate, and those with an average variation greater than 0.33 were considered poor or concerning. In this way, we were able to compare how well the tool aligned with the expert assessments for each construct. For example, if the tool generated a score of 0.03 for Construct 3.1, "PN cooperation with US," for Partner Nation A, and the expert assessment of that construct was low, or 0.17, the absolute variation between the two numbers would be 0.14. An absolute variation of 0.14 would be considered "good," meaning that the tool closely approximated the expert assessment for that construct. Of the 24 constructs, ten, or 42 percent, were noted as good and are highlighted in green in Table B.1.

Only 14 constructs had an average absolute variation between 0.17 and 0.33, which was rated as "moderate." Among those moderately discordant measures, only two also showed a high degree of variation between tool-generated scores and expert assessment scores for individual countries. We calculated this supporting measure by comparing the absolute value of

---

[1] Paul et al., 2013.

[2] One of the original 27 constructs was excluded from this validation analysis. For construct 10.1, "US-PN agreements—information sharing," no measure was identified for the tool, so no validation was necessary.

the difference between the tool score and the expert assessment for each country in each construct to determine how well the tool aligned with expert assessments for individual countries. The two constructs with as many as nine individual country scores higher than 0.33, included Construct 7.3, "PN government legitimacy," and Construct 3.4, "Shared interests between US and PN." These constructs, highlighted in orange in Table B.1, were therefore considered weaker approximation tools. These constructs were downweighted based on the quality of the evidence supporting the hypotheses they represent and the strength of the contributing research.

Of the remaining 12 moderately discordant constructs, only a couple had as many as three individual scores that were higher than 0.5, indicating that there was a high degree of variation between the numbers generated by the tool and our expert assessments for three particular countries for two constructs. We expected these two constructs, 1.1, "US SC/SFA/BPC funding consistent," and 2.2, "Historical success with foreign aid," to be somewhat variable due to the inherent volatility of security force assistance and foreign aid, as well as the difficulty of measuring relative consistency and impact. We also anticipated differences reflecting the fact that the expert assessments could account for nuances of the individual cases that could not be captured in a global, data-driven tool. The measures for these constructs were therefore not downweighted.

It is important to note that in no instance did a construct value have an average absolute variation from the expert assessment greater than 0.33. Therefore, there were no constructs that were deemed to be poor or concerning, on the whole.

Overall, the results of the comparison of the construct scores generated by the tool with those provided independently by SMEs demonstrated that the scores were fairly well aligned and effectively validated the proxy measures used in the tool. In a high percentage of cases, the proxy measures aligned closely with the expert assessments. Moreover, in cases in which there was some discordance between the two scores, the proxy measures were further downweighted based on our perception of their lack of quality. We were thus able to validate the utility of the tool in approximating the measures that are likely to contribute to BPC success.

Table B.1
Results of the Tool Validation Test

Construct	Average Absolute Value of Deviation	Number of Cases with Deviation > 0.33
1.1: US SC/SFA/BPC funding consistent	0.27	6
1.2: US SC/SFA/BPC funding sufficient	0.21	2
2.1: US historical success with SC/BPC/SFA	0.19	4
2.2: Historical success with foreign aid	0.23	5
3.1: PN cooperation with US	0.20	5
3.2: PN citizen perception of US	0.16	2
3.3: Long-term relationship between US and PN	0.15	3
3.4: Shared interests between US and PN	0.26	9
4.1: PN government invests in military	0.19	4
4.2: PN public support for military	0.13	3
5.1: PN military forces' absorptive capacity	0.18	4
5.2: PN absorptive capacity—technical	0.25	6
5.3: PN absorptive capacity—ministerial	0.22	6
6.1: PN government competence/strength	0.14	1
7.1: PN democratic	0.13	0
7.2: PN government stability	0.23	4
7.3: PN government legitimacy	0.29	9
7.4: PN governance	0.12	1
7.5: Lack of PN government corruption	0.14	4
7.6: PN human rights record	0.18	6
8.1: PN economy	0.18	6
9.1: PN security	0.12	0
10.2: US-PN agreements — legal status of US forces	0.26	7
10.3: US-PN common language	0.37	12
10.4: PN transportation infrastructure	0.15	3
10.5: PN communications infrastructure	0.16	4

NOTE: For construct 10.1, "US-PN agreements—information sharing," no measure was identified for the tool, so no validation was necessary.

Mathematical Methods

This appendix describes the mathematical principles and calculations used to determine the individual country scores in the tool, including all measure, construct, category, and overall propensity scores. In short, 66 measures (derived from global data sources) combine to determine 27 construct scores that, in turn, combine to determine ten category scores that, finally, combine to determine the overall propensity scores for 195 potential PNs.[1] As described here, these combinations are based on a system of weights accounting for both the strength of the literary evidence and the quality and relevancy of the data supporting the various measures and constructs.

Mathematical Notation

Before proceeding, we must define the basic mathematical notation used in this appendix. There are four levels of country scores in the tool: measures, constructs, categories, and overall scores. Scores at higher levels are obtained by summing across all subordinate element scores multiplied by their respective weights. We use the letters i, j, and k as indices for the categories, constructs, and measures, respectively:

- Measure_score $[i, j, k]$ = country measure scores for the kth measure in the jth construct in the ith category.
- Construct_score $[i, j]$ = country construct scores for the jth construct in the ith category.
- Category_score $[i]$ = country category scores for the ith category.
- Overall_score = security cooperation propensity score for each country.

All scores range between 0 (worst possible score) and 1 (best possible score). Note that the 66 measures are not distributed evenly among the 27 constructs. Some constructs have as many as eight supporting measures, while others have only one. Similarly, the 27 constructs are not distributed evenly among the ten categories. We use the following notation for the system of weights:

- ω $[i, j, k]$ = measure weight for the kth measure in the jth construct in the ith category.
- μ $[i, j]$ = construct weight for the jth construct in the ith category.
- α $[i]$ = category weight for the ith category.

---

[1] Because of missing data, not all countries can be assigned scores for every measure, construct, and category; however, all 195 countries currently have an overall propensity score.

As discussed next, the measure weights, ω, will vary by country. This is because some country data are missing, and, as such, we cannot define all measures for all countries. In such cases, we set the country measure weight equal to 0. This eliminates the measure from further calculations for countries with missing data. It also shifts the measure weight to the other well-defined measures in the same construct.

Measures

Each measure is derived from one or more global data sources. The first step in defining a measure is to convert the country-level data into a range of values. If a measure has only one data source, then the data provide the country values. However, if a measure has multiple data sources, then we mathematically derive the range of values. For example, Measure 5.1.2, "PN military spending in millions constant US $ per troop," requires both PN annual military expenditures and PN troop levels as data inputs. Here, the country values equal the military expenditures divided by the troop levels. When country values differ by orders of magnitude (as in Measure 5.1.2), we take the logarithm of each value to "smooth" out the distribution.

Next, all measures are scaled between 0 and 1, with 0 and 1 representing the worst and best possible PN measure scores, respectively. This rescaling is a combination of both linear interpolation and percentile rank ordering. Specifically, we linearly interpolate the country values within each quartile.[2] (So, countries with values between the minimum and first quartile receive measure scores between 0.00 and 0.25; countries with values between the first and second quartiles receive measure scores between 0.25 and 0.50.) This approach minimizes the impact of outliers while maintaining a higher correlation between the data and the resulting measure scores. Countries with missing data do not receive a measure score.

Each measure weight is derived subjectively based on how closely the measure approximates the parent construct and the overall quality of the data sources used to compute the measure. These measure weights range from 0 (very poor proxy) to 1 (the perfect proxy). All countries with the necessary data are assigned the same weight (referred to as the standard measure weight). For countries with missing data (and no measure score), we set the measure weight equal to 0. Finally, the standard measure weights are normalized within each construct so that they sum to 1, e.g., $\sum_{k} \omega[i,j,k] = 1$. However, for countries with missing data (and undefined measures in the construct), the equation is $0 \leq \sum_{k} \omega[i,j,k] < 1$.

Constructs

Construct scores are calculated directly from the subordinate measures and their corresponding weights. However, the construct weights are somewhat more complicated than the measure weights because they are a product of both the quality and quantity of the previous research underlying the construct and the quality and relevancy of the data and data sources that define the supporting measures. So, for a construct to have a significant impact on the overall country

---

[2] The first, second, third, and fourth quartiles are equivalent to the 25th, 50th, 75th, and 100th percentiles; the fourth quartile (100th percentile) is also the maximum country value.

scores, it must both be considered highly important in the literature and be supported by high-quality and highly representative data. If either component is lacking, then the construct's impact will diminish relative to the other constructs. For each PN, we compute construct scores as follows:

$$\text{Construct\_score}[i,j] = \frac{\sum_k \omega[i,j,k] \times \text{measure\_score}[i,j,k]}{\sum_k \omega[i,j,k]}.$$

The summation in the denominator renormalizes the measure weights for those measures that are defined for a given PN.[3] If a PN has no valid measures in a construct and $\sum_k \omega[i,j,k] = 0$, then it follows that the construct score is undefined. However, countries with only partially missing data do not necessarily receive lower construct scores as the weights for missing measures shift to the other measures. But, for countries with less and less data supporting a given construct, one should expect the construct's influence on the parent category score and overall score to diminish (as discussed in the next section). For each construct, we define the following variables:

- ρ is the strength of association or correlation between the construct and PN security cooperation success, with $0 \le \rho \le 1$; $\rho = 0$ implies no correlation, and $\rho = 1$ implies perfect correlation.
- Q refers to the quality of previous research supporting. For each construct, we assigned letter grades to the research ranging from A to D. These grades correspond to the following numerical values: 1.00, 0.75, 0.50, and 0.25.
- N is the number of research studies supporting the construct, e.g., $N = 1, 2, 3$.
- R represents the extent to which the construct was deemed redundant or duplicative of other constructs; $R \ge 1$, where $R = 1$ implies that the construct does not overlap with other constructs, and higher values of R imply multiple redundancies with other constructs.

RAND researchers determined three of these variables (ρ, Q, R) using subjective criterion. We define the construct weight component, denoted as τ, that estimates the quality and quantity of previous research verifying each construct:

$$\tau[i,j] = \left(\frac{\rho}{R}\right) \times \min\left(1, Q + 0.25 \times \left(1 - e^{-(N-1)}\right)\right) = (\text{first term}) \times (\text{second term}).$$

If $N = 1$, then the second term equals the research quality grade (Q) and the equation above becomes the product of the correlation strength (ρ) and Q divided by the redundancy variable (R), e.g.,

$$\tau[i,j] = \rho \times \frac{Q}{R}.$$

---

[3]   If all PN measures are defined within the construct (e.g., no missing data), then the denominator equals 1 and there is no need to normalize.

But, as the number of research studies supporting the construct (N) increases, the second term in the equation above increases as well. However, it can only increase by—at most—0.25, or one letter grade, and does not exceed 1.00. A user of the tool can override the formula above by manually inputting these values.[4]

All construct weights have a second component, denoted as δ, that is between 0 and 1 and estimates how well the subordinate measures gauge a particular construct in the aggregate. If a given construct has only one supporting measure, then δ equals the subordinate standard measure weight. However, if there are multiple supporting measures, the construct sum will be at least as large as the largest supporting standard measure weight, and it may be even larger (closer to 1), depending on the number of additional supporting measures, their weights, and their perceived redundancy (the less redundant, the higher the construct sum). Finally, the construct weights, denoted as μ, are products of the two components τ and δ, e.g., $\mu[i, j] = \tau[i, j] \times \delta[i, j]$, incorporating both the existing literary evidence and supporting data quality into the system of weights.

Categories and Overall Scores

We derived each of the ten category scores from the subordinate construct scores and weights in a manner that is similar to the way we derived construct scores from the subordinate measure scores and weights, except that we include an additional summation term, $\sum_k \omega[i, j, k]$, to account for missing data:[5]

$$\text{Category\_score}[i] = \frac{\sum_j \left(\sum_k \omega[i, j, k] \right) \times \mu[i, j] \times \text{construct\_score}[i, j]}{\sum_j \left(\sum_k \omega[i, j, k] \right) \times \mu[i, j]}.$$

If a country is missing data for the *jth* construct, then $\sum_k \omega[i, j, k] < 1$, which effectively reduces the construct weight from $\mu[i, j]$ to

$$\left(\sum_k \omega[i, j, k] \right) \times \mu[i, j].$$

Finally, we define the category weights, α, such that

$$\alpha[i] = \sum_j \left(\sum_k \omega[i, j, k] \right) \times \mu[i, j].$$

It follows that a country's security cooperation propensity score is given by

---

[4]   See the last spreadsheet in the tool, "Category Construct Weights."

[5]   For a country with no defined construct scores in a given category, the category score is also undefined.

$$\text{Overall\_score} = \frac{\sum_i \alpha[i] \times \text{category\_score}[i]}{\sum_i \alpha[i]}.$$

As in the case of the construct weight component, $\tau[i, j]$, the user can override this formula and input his or her own values for the category weights, $\alpha[i]$.

It should be noted that the categories are just a means of grouping similar constructs in order to consolidate the country scoring presentation into a manageable format (ten country category scores plus an overall country propensity score versus 27 country construct scores plus an overall country propensity score). Unless the user inputs his or her own values for the category weights, the categories themselves have no bearing on the overall propensity scores. In fact, the overall country propensity scores can be defined directly from the constructs as follows:

$$\text{Overall\_score} = \frac{\sum_i \sum_j \left(\sum_k \omega[i, j, k]\right) \times \mu[i, j] \times \text{construct\_score}[i, j]}{\sum_i \sum_j \left(\sum_k \omega[i, j, k]\right) \times \mu[i, j]}.$$

Updating the Currency of the Tool

The tool contains 66 individual country measures, which are derived from a wide range of publicly available data sources. Most of these data sources are updated annually, and each new data addition is associated with the year of its release.[1] To maintain the tool's currency, the user must ensure that it contains the most recent versions of the data sets.

Data Updates

There are 12 spreadsheets in the tool that require external data inputs and updates. Ten of these sheets (one for each category), titled "CAT 1 Data & Measure Weights" through "CAT 10 Data & Measure Weights," define the supporting constructs and measures, provide data links and sources, and feature country tables for each measure where the user can update the measure when new data become available. With the exception of the measures in Categories 1 and 2 and Measure 5.3.2 (Category 5), all data updates will be reflected in the specific columns of the measure tables. Some measures require only one column to be updated while others require updates to multiple columns. Figure D.1 shows a partial example of a measure table (Measure 3.1.1) as it appears in the tool.

The cells shaded light yellow with blue font (or sometimes empty) are the data entry cells where the user enters new country-level data when they become available. Measure 3.1.1, "PN troop contributions per capita (millions) to coalition operations, last 10 years, limited to deployments of at least 100 troops," has two data entry columns: one for the PN troop contributions and one for PN population. The remaining cells in Figure D.1 are locked and cannot be altered by the user. The last column, titled "Value," computes PN troop contributions per million people using the data entered in the previous two columns. Hyperlinks to the data sources are provided on the left side of each category sheet under the corresponding construct and measure definitions.

All the measures in Categories 1 and 2 and Measure 5.3.2 (Category 5) require historical data dating prior to the current year. These historical data tables can be found in the "Data Tables" sheet of the tool. There are nine data tables, each containing placeholder columns for future years through 2020. When new country data become available, the user must enter the data into the column under the appropriate year. Each of these measures also requires an additional entry in the measure table heading indicating the current year of the data. Once data have been entered for the next year, the user must update the reference year in the measure

---

[1] All data sources appear to be updated annually, but some do not present the data in a year-by-year table format.

Figure D.1
Example Measure Table

Measure 3.1.1: PN troop contributions per capita (millions) to coalition operations, last 10 years (CPASS)					
#	Country or Territory	ISO	Contributions	PN Pop.	Value
1	Afghanistan	AFG	0	35,320,445	0.0
2	Albania	ALB	1,291	3,215,988	401.4
3	Algeria	DZA	0	35,980,193	0.0
4	Andorra	ADO		86,165	
5	Angola	AGO	0	19,618,432	0.0
6	Antigua and Barbuda	ATG		89,612	
7	Argentina	ARG	7,818	40,764,561	191.8
8	Armenia	ARM	0	3,100,236	0.0
9	Australia	AUS	20,266	22,620,600	895.9
10	Austria	AUT	10,608	8,419,000	1,260.0
11	Azerbaijan	AZE	300	9,168,000	32.7
12	Bahamas	BHS		347,000	
13	Bahrain	BHR	0	1,323,535	0.0
14	Bangladesh	BGD	75,106	150,493,658	499.1
15	Barbados	BRB		273,925	
16	Belarus	BLR	0	9,473,000	0.0
17	Belgium	BEL	9,874	11,008,000	897.0

Data entered by user

table heading in order to incorporate the new data into the measure calculations. Figure D.2 provides an example of a measure requiring reference year input in the measure table heading (Measure 5.3.2). These cells are also shaded yellow with blue, underlined font. Note that, in some cases (Categories 1 and 2), the measures draw on multiple data tables and thus require multiple reference year updates.

Data Entry Tips

Most, if not all, of the data sources in the tool are updated annually, but they may be updated at different times during the year. So, to keep the tool current, the user may have to periodically visit the various data sources, checking to see whether new data have recently become available. Most data sources are in tabular format, making the data entry into Excel much easier. However, not all (if any) of the data sources cover the exact same 195 countries as the tool. Moreover, not all data sources use the same naming conventions for each country (e.g., Burma versus Myanmar), which alters the PN ordering. We found that the easiest data entry approach

Figure D.2
Example Reference Year Input Value with Measure Table Heading

Measure 5.3.2: GDP per capita growth, average over last 5 years (World Bank)				
#	**Country or Territory**	**ISO**	**Current data year for GDP per Capita growth (Data Table #8)** 2011	**Value**
1	Afghanistan	AFG		7.75
2	Albania	ALB		4.28
3	Algeria	DZA		1.18
4	Andorra	ADO		0.80
5	Angola	AGO		6.08
6	Antigua and Barbuda	ATG		-7.28
7	Argentina	ARG		5.92
8	Armenia	ARM		2.44
9	Australia	AUS		0.80
10	Austria	AUT		0.98
11	Azerbaijan	AZE		8.54
12	Bahamas	BHS		-2.12
13	Bahrain	BHR		-5.45
14	Bangladesh	BGD		5.04
15	Barbados	BRB		-1.73
16	Belarus	BLR		7.00
17	Belgium	BEL		0.20

Current/latest year of data in Data Table #8 entered by user

is to first copy and paste the country names and source data into a temporary spreadsheet and then copy and paste an alphabetized list of the 195 countries from the tool next to the country names and source data. The user can then physically align the country data with the tool's list of countries by hand. Once aligned, the new data can be pasted directly into the tool.

In most cases, an external database will not contain data for all 195 countries. The general rule is that when data are missing, the corresponding country cells should be left blank. However, there are exceptions to this rule:

- If the user believes that missing data implies a specific value, then that value can be entered in lieu of leaving the cell blank. For example, for U.S. military assistance data (see Data Table 4 in the tool), we assumed that missing data implied that the United States did not provide military assistance to that country during that year and subsequently entered a value of 0.
- If older data are available (within five years of the current data) and the user believes that the older data would serve as a good proxy for the current data, he or she can input the older (most recent) data.
- If the user can accurately estimate the data, then these results can be entered in the data cells as well. For example, not all PN GDP data (see Data Table 1 in the tool) were avail-

able back to 2001. In some cases, we estimated the values using alternative data sources or other data, such as annual GDP growth, when available.

In short, when the user believes good proxy data are available, he or she should use the proxy data instead of leaving the cells blank.

Only the measures in Categories 1 and 2 and Measure 5.3.2 are linked to the data tables in the "Data Tables" tab. Many of the remaining measures use the same current-year data contained in the data tables. However, these measures are not linked to the data tables. Instead, the same current-year data must be copied and pasted into the correct column of the measure table. In some cases, as for PN GDP, multiple measures that are not linked to the data tables require the same data. As such, the user must enter new data in multiple measure tables, in addition to Data Table 1 ("PN GDP in constant US $ [World Bank]").

Strategy and Policy Consideration Data

The "Strategy & Policy Considerations" tab looks and works very similarly to the ten category sheets. Each strategy and policy consideration is defined on the left side of the spreadsheet, along with sources and data links. And, as in the case of the category measures, the user must make the requisite updates whenever new data become available. Note that some of the data required in this sheet are duplicative of the data required in the category sheets.

Bibliography

Bipartisan Policy Center, *Fragility and Extremism in Yemen*, Washington, D.C., February 2010. As of May 15, 2013:
http://bipartisanpolicy.org/sites/default/files/Yemen%20Fragility%20and%20Extremism.pdf

Bissell, J. B., "Never Lost in Translation: With the U.S. Armed Forces a Constant Presence Around the World, the Need for Professional, Military Linguists Has Never Been Greater," *Military Advanced Education Journal*, Vol. 6, No. 2, March 2011, pp. 6–9. As of May 15, 2013:
http://www.kmimediagroup.com/files/MAE_6-2_Final.pdf

Budney, Michael, John Dziminowicz, and Erwann Michel-Kerjan, *Enhancing Theater Security Cooperation in the 21st Century: How the U.S. Navy Can Help*, Philadelphia, Pa.: Risk Management and Decision Processes Center, Wharton School, University of Pennsylvania, January 2008. As of May 15, 2013:
http://opim.wharton.upenn.edu/risk/library/WP2008-01-02_MB,JD,EMK_TSC_Navy.pdf

Caldwell, William B. IV, and Nathan K. Finney, "Building Police Capacity in Afghanistan: The Challenges of a Multilateral Approach," *Prism*, Vol. 2, No. 1, December 2010, pp. 121–130. As of May 15, 2013:
http://www.ndu.edu/press/building-police-capacity-in-afghanistan.html

Defense Security Cooperation Agency, *DSCA Campaign Support Plan 2010*, Arlington, Va.: January 1, 2010. As of May 15, 2013:
http://www.dsca.mil/programs/Program_Support/DSCA%20CSP%20no%20names.pdf

———, "Frequently Asked Questions (FAQs)," web page, last updated August 15, 2012. As of May 15, 2013:
http://www.dsca.mil/PressReleases/faq.htm

Flickinger, Robert T., *Integrating Intelligence and Information Sharing in Theater Security Cooperation*, Newport, R.I.: U.S. Naval War College, May 4, 2009. As of May 15, 2013:
http://www.dtic.mil/cgi-bin/GetTRDoc?AD=ADA502913

Gates, Robert M., "Helping Others Defend Themselves," *Foreign Affairs*, Vol. 89, No. 3, May–June 2010.

Gelman, Andrew, John B. Carlin, Hal S. Stern, and Donald B. Rubin, *Bayesian Data Analysis*, Boca Raton, Fla.: Chapman and Hall, 1995.

Headquarters, U.S. Department of the Army, *Stability Operations*, Field Manual 3-07, Washington, D.C., October 6, 2008.

Institute for Defense Analyses, "Analysis of Selected Historical Security Force Assistance Engagements," unpublished briefing, June 15, 2011.

Joint Center for International Security Force Assistance, *Commander's Handbook for Security Force Assistance*, Fort Leavenworth, Kan., July 14, 2008. As of May 15, 2013:
http://usacac.army.mil/cac2/Repository/Materials/SFA.pdf

Kilcullen, David J., "Three Pillars of Counterinsurgency," remarks delivered at the U.S. Government Counterinsurgency Conference, Washington, D.C., September 28, 2006. As of May 15, 2013:
http://www.au.af.mil/au/awc/awcgate/uscoin/3pillars_of_counterinsurgency.pdf

Livingston, Thomas K., *Building the Capacity of Partner States Through Security Force Assistance*, Washington, D.C.: Congressional Research Service, May 5, 2011.

Marshall, Jeffery E., *Skin in the Game: Partnership in Establishing and Maintaining Global Security and Stability,* Washington, D.C.: National Defense University Press, 2011.

Marquis, Jefferson P., Jennifer D. P. Moroney, Justin Beck, Derek Eaton, Scott Hiromoto, David R. Howell, Janet Lewis, Charlotte Lynch, Michael J. Neumann, and Cathryn Quantic Thurston, *Developing an Army Strategy for Building Partner Capacity for Stability Operations,* Santa Monica, Calif.: RAND Corporation, MG-942-A, 2010. As of May 15, 2013:
http://www.rand.org/pubs/monographs/MG942.html

Maxwell, Dayton, and Mark Sweberg, "Comprehensive Approach to Building Partnerships Handbook and Reference Guide," presentation at Cornwallis Group Workshop on Analysis for Future Conflict, St. Leonhard Uberlingen, Germany, March 28–April 1, 2011. As of May 15, 2013:
http://www.thecornwallisgroup.org/workshop_2011.php

McKenzie, Kenneth F., and Elizabeth C. Packard, "Enduring Interests and Partnerships: Military-to-Military Relationships and the Arab Spring," *Prism,* Vol. 3, No. 1, December 2011, pp. 99–106. As of May 15, 2013:
http://www.ndu.edu/press/relationships-in-the-arab-spring.html

Midgley, Jack, "Building Partner Capability: Defining an Army Role in Future Small Wars," *Small Wars Journal,* February 20, 2012. As of May 15, 2013:
http://smallwarsjournal.com/jrnl/art/building-partner-capability

Moroney, Jennifer D. P., Adam Grissom, and Jefferson P. Marquis, *A Capabilities-Based Strategy for Army Security Cooperation,* Santa Monica, Calif.: RAND Corporation, MG-563-A, 2007. As of May 15, 2013:
http://www.rand.org/pubs/monographs/MG563.html

Moroney, Jennifer D. P., Joe Hogler, Benjamin Bahney, Kim Cragin, David R. Howell, Charlotte Lynch, and S. Rebecca Zimmerman, *Building Partner Capacity to Combat Weapons of Mass Destruction,* Santa Monica, Calif.: RAND Corporation, MG-783-DTRA, 2009. As of May 15, 2013:
http://www.rand.org/pubs/monographs/MG783.html

Norris, John, and Connie Veillette, *Engagement Amid Austerity: A Bipartisan Approach to Reorienting the International Affairs Budget,* Washington, D.C.: Center for American Progress and Center for Global Development, May 2012. As of May 15, 2013:
http://www.cgdev.org/files/1426170_file_Norris_Veillette_austerity.pdf

O'Mahoney, Angela, Derek Eaton, Michael J. McNerney, and Thomas S. Szayna, "Assessing Security Cooperation as a Preventive Tool: Preliminary Observations," unpublished RAND briefing, March 2012.

Palmer, Jeffrey S., "Legal Impediments to USAFRICOM Operationalization," *Joint Force Quarterly,* No. 51, 4th Quarter 2008, pp. 79–86. As of May 15, 2013:
http://www.dtic.mil/cgi-bin/GetTRDoc?Location=U2&doc=GetTRDoc.pdf&AD=ADA518763

Paul, Christopher, Colin P. Clarke, Beth Grill, Stephanie Young, Jennifer D. P. Moroney, Joe Hogler, and Christine Leah, *What Works Best When Building Partner Capacity and Under What Circumstances?* Santa Monica, Calif.: RAND Corporation, MG-1253/1-OSD, 2013. As of May 15, 2013:
http://www.rand.org/pubs/monographs/MG1253z1.html

Schear, James A., William B. Caldwell IV, and Frank C. Digiovanni, "Ministerial Advisors: Developing Capacity for an Enduring Security Force," *Prism,* Vol. 2, No. 2, March 2011, pp. 135–144. As of May 15, 2013:
http://www.ndu.edu/press/ministerial-advisors-enduring-security-force.html

Serafino, Nina M., *Security Assistance Reform: "Section 1206" Background and Issues for Congress,* Washington, D.C.: Congressional Research Service, April 19, 2012.

Shadish, William R., "The Logic of Generalization: Five Principles Common to Experiments and Ethnographies," *American Journal of Community Psychology,* Vol. 23, No. 3, June 1995, pp. 419–428.

Sullivan, Patricia L., Brock F. Tessman, and Xiaojun Li, "U.S. Military Aid and Recipient State Cooperation," *Foreign Policy Analysis,* Vol. 7, No. 3, July 2011, pp. 275–294.

Terry, Jason B., *Principles of Building Partnership Capacity,* thesis, Fort Leavenworth, Kan.: U.S. Army Command and General Staff College, 2010. As of May 15, 2013:
http://www.au.af.mil/au/awc/awcgate/army/cgsc_bldg_partner_capacity_nov2010.pdf

Teichert, E. John, "The Building Partner Capacity Imperative," *DISAM Journal*, Vol. 31-2, August 2009, pp. 116–125. As of May 15, 2013:
http://www.disam.dsca.mil/pubs/Indexes/Vol%2031_2/Teichert.pdf

Thaler, David E., Jefferson P. Marquis, and Jennifer D. P. Moroney, "FY10 Building Partnerships Project Prioritization Construct," unpublished RAND briefing, November 2010.

U.S. Agency for International Development, *U.S. Overseas Loans and Grants, Obligations, and Loan Authorizations (Greenbook)*, Washington, D.C., various years.

U.S. Code, Title 22, Section 2304, Human Rights and Security Assistance.

U.S. Department of Defense, *Building Partnership Capacity: QDR Execution Roadmap*, Washington, D.C., May 22, 2006. As of May 15, 2013:
http://www.ndu.edu/itea/storage/790/BPC%20Roadmap.pdf

———, *Quadrennial Defense Review Report*, Washington, D.C., February 2010.

———, *Sustaining U.S. Global Leadership: Priorities for 21st Century Defense*, Washington, D.C., January 2012a.

———, *Security Assistance Management Manual (SAMM)*, Washington, D.C., DoD 5105.38-M, April 30, 2012b. As of September 24, 2012:
http://www.dsca.mil/SAMM

U.S. Department of Defense Instruction 5000.68, *Security Force Assistance (SFA)*, October 27, 2010.

Veneri, Michael C., "The Partner Predicament: U.S. Building Partnership Capacity, the War on Terrorism and What the U.S. Cannot Overlook," *Synesis*, Vol. 2, 2011, pp. G:7–G:17. As of September 17, 2012:
http://www.synesisjournal.com/vol2_g/2011_2_G7-17_Veneri.pdf

Data Sources

Amnesty International, Political Terror Scale, 1978–2008. As of January 21, 2013:
http://politicalterrorscale.org/about.php

Center for Systemic Peace, Integrated Network for Societal Conflict Research, data files on major episodes of political violence, 2008. As of January 21, 2013:
http://www.systemicpeace.org/inscr/inscr.htm

Center for Systemic Peace, Integrated Network for Societal Conflict Research, Polity IV Project, data files on political regime characteristics and transitions, 2011. As of January 21, 2013:
http://www.systemicpeace.org/inscr/inscr.htm

Center for Systemic Peace, Integrated Network for Societal Conflict Research, State Fragility Index, data files on political legitimacy subindex, 2011. As of January 21, 2013:
http://www.systemicpeace.org/inscr/inscr.htm

Central Intelligence Agency, World Fact Book, data files on GDP in current U.S. dollars, percentage of population living in poverty, official language, 2012. As of January 18, 2013:
https://www.cia.gov/library/publications/the-world-factbook

Congressional Research Service, *Status of Forces Agreement (SOFA): What Is It, and How Has It Been Utilized?* Washington, D.C., March 15, 2012. As of January 21, 2013:
http://www.fas.org/sgp/crs/natsec/index.html

Gallup World View, data files on the survey question, "Do you approve or disapprove of the job performance of the leadership of the United States?" 2012. As of January 18, 2013 (registration required):
https://worldview.gallup.com/default.aspx

Georgetown University, Center for Security Studies, data files on troop contributions to military operations, 2001–2011. As of January 18, 2013:
http://css.georgetown.edu/research/focus/peacekeeping/troops/

Global Peace Index, 2012. As of January 18, 2013:
http://www.visionofhumanity.org/gpi-data/

Index Mundi, data files on GDP in current US dollars, 2012. As of January 18, 2013:
http://www.indexmundi.com/factbook/countries

Institute for Economics and Peace, Global Peace Index, data files on military capability, conflicts fought, organized conflict (internal), violent demonstrations, neighboring country relations, 2012. As of January 18, 2013:
http://www.visionofhumanity.org/gpi-data

Institute of International Education, Open Doors Report on International Educational Exchange data files on host regions and destinations of U.S. study abroad students and international students studying in the United States, by place of origin, 2012. As of January 18, 2013:
http://www.iie.org/Research-and-Publications/Open-Doors/Data

International Monetary Fund (IMF), World Economic Outlook Database, data files on GDP per capita, 2012. As of January 21, 2013:
http://www.imf.org/external/pubs/ft/weo/2012/02/weodata/index.aspx

Jane's Country Risk Intelligence Centre Module, data files on involvement with multilateral institutions, efficacy of security forces, professionalism of security forces, state control of security forces, internal stability, external stability, 2011. As of January 18, 2013:
http://www.janes.com (login required)

Leeds, Brett Ashley, Jeffrey M. Ritter, Sara McLaughlin Mitchell, and Andrew G. Long, *Alliance Treaty Obligations and Provisions, 1815–1944*, International Interactions 28, 2002, pp. 237–260. As of January 18, 2013:
http://atop.rice.edu/download/ATOPcdbk.pdf and http://atop.rice.edu/download/data/ATOP3_0basiccsv.zip

Legatum Institute, Legatum Prosperity Index, data files on economy subindex, 2012. As of January 21, 2013:
http://www.prosperity.com

Lewis, M. Paul, ed., *Ethnologue: Languages of the World*, 16th ed., Dallas, Tex.: SIL International, 2009. As of January 21, 2013:
http://www.ethnologue.com/

Mayer, Thierry, and Soledad Zignago, notes on CEPII's distances measures (GeoDist), Centre D'Etudes Prospectives et d'Informations Internationales Working Paper 2011-25, 2011. As of January 18, 2013:
http://www.cepii.com/anglaisgraph/bdd/distances.htm

National Geospatial-Intelligence Agency, data files on C-130/C-17–compatible runways, not available to the general public.

Organisation for Economic Co-operation and Development, data files on total foreign aid to all countries in current U.S. dollars, 2012. As of January 18, 2013:
http://stats.oecd.org/qwids

SIPRI—*see* Stockholm International Peace Research Institute.

Stockholm International Peace Research Institute, Arms Transfers Database, data files on arms transfers from Russia and China, 2010–2012. As of January 21, 2013:
http://www.sipri.org/databases/armstransfers

———, Military Expenditure Database, data files on military expenditures, 2011. As of January 18, 2013 (registration required):
http://www.sipri.org/databases/milex

Transparency International, data files on corruption perceptions index, 2011. As of January 21, 2013:
http://www.transparency.org/research/cpi/

United Nations Department of Peacekeeping Operations, data files on troop contributions to United Nations peacekeeping operations, 2012. As of January 18, 2013:
http://www.un.org/en/peacekeeping/resources/statistics/contributors.shtml

United Nations Development Programme, *Human Development Report 2011 Sustainability and Equity: A Better Future for All*, New York: Palgrave Macmillan, 2011. As of January 18, 2013:
http://hdr.undp.org/en/reports/global/hdr2011/download

U.S. Agency for International Development, *U.S. Overseas Loans and Grants, Obligations, and Loan Authorizations (Greenbook)*, data files for total obligations of U.S. military assistance in constant 2010 U.S. dollars, 2012. As of January 18, 2013:
http://gbk.eads.usaidallnet.gov

U.S. Department of Commerce, Bureau of the Census, Foreign Trade Division, data files on U.S. trade, by country, 2012. As of January 18, 2013:
http://www.census.gov/foreign-trade/balance

U.S. Department of Commerce, International Trade Administration, Office of Travel and Tourism Industries, *U.S. International Air Travel Calendar Year 2006*, Washington, D.C., 2006. As of January 18, 2013:
http://tinet.ita.doc.gov/research/programs/i92/2006_I92_Air_Travel_Statistics.pdf

U.S. Department of Homeland Security, *2011 Yearbook of Immigration Statistics*, Washington, D.C., 2011. As of January 18, 2013:
http://www.dhs.gov/yearbook-immigration-statistics

U.S. Bureau of Economic Analysis, data files on U.S. direct investment position abroad and foreign direct investment in the United States on a historical-cost basis in U.S. dollars, 2011. As of January 18, 2013: http://www.bea.gov/iTable/index_MNC.cfm

U.S. Department of State, *2012 Adherence to and Compliance with Arms Control, Nonproliferation, and Disarmament Agreements and Commitments*, Washington, D.C., 2012. As of January 21, 2013: http://www.state.gov/t/avc/rls/rpt/c54051.htm

———, *Treaties in Force: A List of Treaties and Other International Agreements of the United States in Force on January 1, 2012*, Washington, D.C., January 1, 2012. As of January 21, 2013: http://www.state.gov/s/l/treaty/tif/index.htm

———, data files on countries determined by the Secretary of State to have repeatedly provided support for acts of international terrorism, 2013. As of January 21, 2013: http://www.state.gov/j/ct/list/c14151.htm

U.S. Department of State, Bureau of Consular Affairs, data files on countries with which the U.S. has a treaty of commerce or navigation allowing either treaty trader (E-1) or treaty investor (E-2) visas. As of January 18, 2013: http://travel.state.gov/visa/fees/fees_3726.html

U.S. Department of State, Bureau of International Organizations, *Voting Practices in the United Nations, 2011, General Assembly: Important Resolutions and Consensus Actions*, Washington, D.C., April 1, 2012. As of January 18, 2013: http://www.state.gov/documents/organization/162417.pdf

U.S. Patent and Trademark Office, data files on utility patents by U.S. state and country of origin, 2011. As of January 21, 2013: http://www.uspto.gov/web/offices/ac/ido/oeip/taf/cst_utl.htm

World Economic Forum, *Global Competitiveness Report 2012–2013*, Geneva, Switzerland, 2012. As of January 21, 2013: http://www.wcforum.org/issues/global-competitiveness

———, *Global Gender Gap Report 2012*, Geneva, Switzerland, 2012. As of January 21, 2013: http://www.weforum.org/issues/global-gender-gap

World Values Survey, data files on confidence in armed forces by country, 2008. As of January 18, 2013: http://www.wvsevsdb.com/wvs/WVSAnalizeQuestion.jsp

World Bank, World Governance Indicators, data files on government effectiveness, regulatory quality, rule of law, political stability, and absence of violence, 2011. As of January 18, 2013: http://info.worldbank.org/governance/wgi/index.asp

———, World Development Indicators, data files on GDP in current U.S. dollars, total armed forces personnel, GDP per capita annual growth rate in U.S. dollars, total population, royalty and license fee balance of payments in U.S. dollars, secondary enrollment ratio, adult literacy rate, tertiary enrollment ratio railways goods transported (million ton-km) per 100,000 people, air transport freight (million ton-km) per 100,000 people, quality of port infrastructure, telephone lines per 100 people, cell phone subscriptions per 100 people, and Internet users per 100 people, 2012. As of January 18, 2013: http://data.worldbank.org